The Long Trail

Mother, Dad, and Carlton a few months before the start of their journey to Grouard, 1912.

The Long Trail

The Story of a Pioneer Family

Beulah Baldwin

NeWest Press

Canadian Cataloguing in Publication Data

Baldwin, Beulah, 1913-
  The long trail

  ISBN 0-920897-23-1

  I. Freeland family. 2. Alberta – Frontier
and pioneer life. 3. Alberta – Biography.
4. Baldwin, Beulah, 1913-   I. Title.
FG3672.1.F74B34 1992   971.23'02'092
F1078.B34 1992   C92-091455-1

Credits:
COVER DESIGN: Diane Jensen
INTERIOR DESIGN: Bob Young/BOOKENDS DESIGNWORKS
EDITOR FOR THE PRESS: Eva Radford
FINANCIAL ASSISTANCE: NeWest Press gratefully acknowledges the
financial assistance of Alberta Culture and Multiculturalism, The Alberta
Foundation for the Arts, The Canada Council, and The NeWest Institute
for Western Canadian Studies.

Printed and bound in Canada by Best Gagné Book Manufacturers.

NeWest Publishers Limited
Suite 310, 10359-82 Avenue
Edmonton, Alberta
T6E 1Z9

To Ged, my husband and my friend,
who reached the end of his trail, December 16, 1991,
this book is lovingly dedicated.

CONTENTS

ACKNOWLEDGMENTS

As a child listening to my parents talk of their adventures along the Grouard Trail, I never thought of them as remarkable people. Nor did they see themselves as anything but ordinary.

It was only after I was grown, and later when I was working on this book, that I began to recognize them, and their contemporaries, for what they were. True pioneers! People with the courage and fortitude to follow their dreams. They came and, more importantly, they endured, staying to settle a new land. It would be their children, and those who came later, who reaped the real benefits of their endeavours.

So many helped me with this book. Unfortunately, I have room to thank only a few: James MacGregor, whose wonderful books, *Blankets and Beads* and *The Land of Twelve Foot Davis*, I have drawn on extensively; Will Marx for his help and whose book, *Grouard-Peace River Trail*, provided a wealth of research material; the service clubs and historical organizations of many northern Alberta towns who provided such a great service to future generations by painstakingly gathering and publishing the stories of their pioneers – *I Remember Peace River, Peace River Remembers,* and High Prairie's *Pioneers Who Blazed the Trail,* are just three of the many books that space allows me to mention here; the Provincial Archives of Alberta, with special thanks to Senior Archivist David Leonard; my friends and family who helped and encouraged me, particularly my daughter-in-law, Pearl, and my daughter, Barbara, for their editing assistance; and a special thanks to Eva Radford.

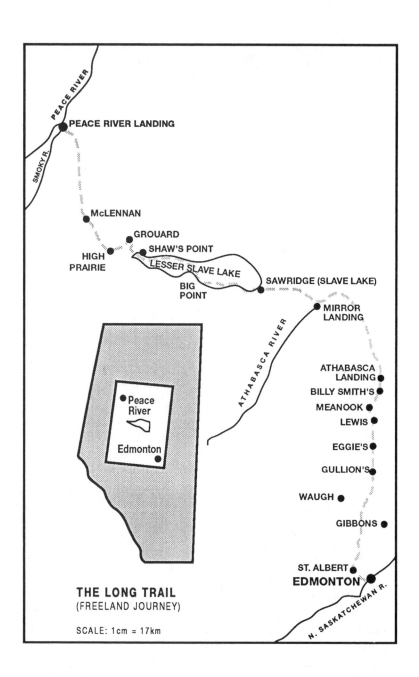

THE LONG TRAIL
(FREELAND JOURNEY)

SCALE: 1cm = 17km

CHAPTER ONE

The Harness Jingles

The big freight sleigh was packed and ready to move out, and my father's team of Clydesdales stamped restlessly in their harnesses, puffing great clouds of steam into the frosty air. Dad whistled as he made his final preparations, fixing the canvas coverings on the sleigh and rechecking the family's belongings and supplies.

Dad was full of music. In later years his family would recognize that his whistle could cover a variety of emotions, but on that bright February morning it meant he was both anxious and excited – excited at the prospect of the journey and the start of a new life for himself and his young wife and child, anxious about the three-hundred-mile trip that lay ahead. He was well aware of the dangers and hardships of the winter journey north over the Athabasca Trail from Edmonton to the pioneer settlement of Grouard.

The year was 1913. Edmonton, a northern city situated in the Province of Alberta, Canada, was experiencing a slump after a terrific boom that had brought thousands of newcomers from the eastern provinces, the United States, and Europe. Among them were my parents, Wilbur and Olive Freeland. They had bought a small hotel on the south side of the Saskatchewan River in the Strathcona District. My young mother, who before her marriage rarely ventured outside the limits of her hometown of Buffalo, New York, had been mainly responsible for the operation of the hotel. Dad had worked as a freighter carting goods and supplies to the tiny new settlements along the Athabasca Trail. Now this young family was joining the growing stream of pioneers leaving Edmonton to seek a new life in the fabled Peace River Country.

Their route lay north along the Athabasca Trail to the settlement of Athabasca Landing, then two hundred miles west over the frozen length of Lesser Slave Lake, to the town of Grouard where Dad had purchased another hotel.

There were two other routes – by the railway, which had been completed as far as Athabasca Landing, or by water on one of the many commercial boats that plied a network of lakes and rivers. But they were costly, and most pioneers opted for the land route, travelling during the winter months when the lakes, rivers, and muskeg were frozen.

Winter is harsh in this northern land where temperatures can drop to minus 60° F or more. Horses had been known to drop dead from frozen lungs, and caravans of two or more outfits always travelled together for safety. Travelling with my parents would be Sam Simpson, a friend of Dad's who had freighted with him. But Sam would not leave until the next day, catching up with them at the village of St. Albert nine miles north of Edmonton.

Although Dad had travelled the trail as far as Athabasca Landing during the two years he had worked as a freighter, he could not help but worry how his young pregnant wife and eighteen-month-old son Carlton would endure the long, tedious hours sitting cramped and cold in the horse-drawn sleigh, and the discomfort of primitive accommodations along the way. He had tried to persuade her to go as far as Athabasca Landing by rail. "It would give you a break for the first one hundred miles," he argued. But she refused, saying, "The baby and I will still have to travel two hundred miles by horse and sleigh, and we might just as well all leave together." Although I was not to join them for another five months, I too was a concern to my parents.

Dad need not have worried. The young woman who stood

watching from the upstairs window had a look of determination and courage in her sparkling blue eyes. She was small, just an inch or two over five feet, with golden brown hair piled high on her head. When her husband looked up and waved for her to join him, she waved back, and the answering smile that broke across her face made her truly beautiful.

Mother descended the stairs slowly, helping Carlton, who was so bundled up he could barely move. Finally, in her impatience, she scooped him up and lugged him toward the sleigh. Dad rushed to meet them. He swung them up onto the broad, high-backed seat that she had helped him pad with old pillows from their hotel. They had covered it with a red Hudson's Bay blanket, setting off the beautiful buffalo robe Dad bought from an Indian during his last freighting trip.

Before Mother settled her self and the baby, Dad pulled aside the sleigh's canvas covering, saying, "Look Ollie." She smiled, observing the cosy nest he had arranged in the back so that she and Carlton could rest, safe from the cold winds. Dad had spent hours making the canvas covering that extended over the back of the rig and partially over the seat. Their clothes and other personal belongings, including Mother's fine china, photographs and other treasures she had brought from her home in Buffalo, were carefully arranged in the back. They also packed prepared food, staples, and feed for the team, in the event they were forced to spend the night at a stopping house that lacked proper accommodation and facilities.

Sam had come to see them off. He suddenly darted to his sleigh and returned with a bale of hay which he placed under Mother's feet, saying with a smile, "My going away present." It made a perfect footstool for her short legs, and she would remember his thoughtfulness many times during the journey.

My parents' friends had given them a goodbye party the previous night and, not wanting to prolong the sadness of goodbyes, Mother and Dad now hoped no one would come to see them off. But just as Dad picked up the reins, John and Elsie Henderson appeared with their little girl, Beulah. Mother loved Beulah; many times she had wondered how she could have coped during busy periods at the hotel, if the child had not been there to amuse Carlton. Now her little friend held up a box of cookies she had baked, tears streaming down her freckled face. Mother reached down and lifted the little girl into her lap, hugging her as they both wept. Carlton also burst into tears at the unhappiness of the two people most important to his little world. When I was born five months later, I was named Beulah after this child who meant so much to my mother.

"Look," said Sam, pointing to the window above. Brownie, my parents' beautiful red setter stood on her hind legs with such a mournful expression at being left behind, that tears were quickly forgotten as everyone burst into laughter. Dad had bought Brownie when she was only a few weeks old, hoping she would become a watchdog, but his real intention had been to take Mother's mind off her homesickness. Brownie was leaving with Sam the next day. Their other dog, Trixie, was also sad at being left behind. Trixie, a fox terrier so tiny that when Dad brought him home as a puppy he fit into the bib pocket of Dad's overalls, would not be joining them for several months. Sam helped Beulah out of the sleigh, saying, "Let's you and I go upstairs and cheer up the dogs."

At last the family was ready to go. A shouted goodbye to the Hendersons and Sam, a crack of the whip, and they were off. Babe and Girlie, Dad's matched team, sensed the excitement and broke into a fast trot that soon brought them to the open countryside. They were not built for speed, though, and shortly settled down to their normal fast walk.

The road gradually became a narrow trail, not quite wide enough for two rigs to pass. Mother wanted to know the rules of the road. Dad obliged, saying, "Heavy loads gave half of the road when passing each other, while light rigs with light loads gave all of the road when meeting a heavy load."

"But Wilbur, how can you be sure?" she asked.

He answered with a laugh. "The size of the driver had a lot to do with my judgement."

They left Edmonton behind and soon approached the first farm. Neat white buildings with green roofs stood before a bluff of spruce and birch, protection from the north wind. In a short while they were passing another fine group of buildings. "I've been told," Dad said, "that these well-to-do farmers have homes as fine as any in the city." Mother agreed, saying, "You're right Wilbur, I'd never have believed it." Watching her out of the corner of his eye as they approached the next farm, he was not surprised when she exclaimed, "Their first home!" while pointing out a small log cabin with a sod roof. They were soon passing the farms of the more recent settlers. Although they were not as large or elaborate; built mostly of neatly dove-tailed logs, the small windows were bright and clean and hung with gay curtains. These small homes appealed to Mother. Looking up with a bright smile, she said, "Wouldn't it be fun to peek inside and see how these women have managed to create comfortable homes, with very little to work with?"

She glanced proudly at the warm patchwork quilts she had made from clothing left behind by customers at their hotel – woolen jackets and shirts, tossed carelessly aside by men anxious to leave for a warmer climate and an easier way of life. Like many thrifty wives of that era, she cut the material into small squares, creating a checkerboard pattern, and lined the quilts with carded wool that Dad purchased from Father Lacombe's mission. Sewn by hand, the coverings had taken many months to complete.

Late in the afternoon, just as they reached St. Albert, the lowering sun broke through the cloud cover, lighting the windows of the impressive frame buildings of the mission on a hill overlooking the village and the Sturgeon River. It was a welcome sight to Mother, cramped and cold from holding the sleeping child.

St. Albert was a bustling village with several good hotels established to cater to the ever-increasing number of pioneers following the Athabasca Trail. My parents had been invited to spend the night at the mission. This invitation was the outcome of a friendship between my father and one of the priests who, grateful when Dad rushed an important shipment of supplies to him, had insisted the family spend their first night on the trail as guests of the bishop's residence. Dad had been delighted to accept, knowing Mother would be interested in inspecting the school operated for Native children by the Grey Nuns, as well as learning more of Father Lacombe.

Dad felt a special kinship with this intrepid little priest, who had arrived at Fort Edmonton in 1852 when he was just twenty-five years old and devoted the rest of his life to the Natives of the land he came to love so well. Carrying his banner – a red cross on a white background – to the distant outreaches of the vast north, Father Lacombe cared for the sick and the poor, bringing the word of God to every tribe. It had been his dream to establish a mission for the Indians and Métis where they could receive instructions to help them bridge the gap between the old ways and the new.

In 1860 he began to direct construction of a mission overlooking the Sturgeon River near Fort Edmonton, completing the work with exceptional speed. For many years, there was nothing to equal it in the north. Now Native boys and girls, clad in neat uniforms, received instruction in academic subjects as well as in such practical fields as sewing, weaving, and dairying for the girls, and harness-making, carpentry, and smithing for the boys.

As the mission's mother superior, a small vigorous woman with a French accent and keen, dark, eyes, came to welcome my parents, Mother felt her weariness slip away. They were given comfortable quarters in the bishop's residence and an excellent meal. To my parent's surprise, Carlton was the center of attraction. To many of the dark-skinned pupils, a blond, blue-eyed child was still a novelty.

My parents had arranged to meet Sam at his hotel next morning. Before they left the mission, two nuns came to wish them godspeed and handed them a box of sandwiches, cut from their freshly-baked bread, and cookies baked by the students. The mother superior also took time from her busy schedule to offer prayers for a safe journey.

They found Sam in excellent spirits. He had made good time on the trail. That morning he had fed Brownie and taken her for a run as the weather was mild. He was anxious to head for Morinville about twelve miles away. They had decided to stop there for lunch, then on to St. Emil where they would spend the night.

That evening, beside the St. Emil hotel's big parlour stove, they filled Sam in on the information they had acquired and told him the fascinating and little-known story of Father Lacombe, as related to them by one of the older priests the night before.

Lacombe's ancestors were among Canada's earliest pioneers, helping to clear the forests for the rich farmlands along the wide banks of the St. Lawrence River in the parish of St. Sulpice, Quebec. In those days fish and game were in abundance, although bears were a constant threat. Also, nearly every family had some encounter with raiding Indians, resulting in capture, or loss of life. Fear was part of their everyday existence.

One fall day, Albert Lacombe's great-grandparents were working at the edge of the forest, their guns within easy reach. The younger children had been left at home with their sixteen-year-old daughter, who had been given instructions to stay near the house and sound the alarm if the feared Iroquois were seen. What happened that day was not fully known until many years later, but when the parents returned they found the younger children very frightened and their oldest daughter gone.

One of the girl's uncles was a fur trader whose route took him many miles along the main waterways leading west to Montreal. Some five years after his niece had disappeared, the man pulled his canoe to shore to spend the night trading with an Ojibway band. Before long he noticed a young woman nursing her baby and watching him very closely. Two or three times their glances met before he recognized her as his niece. Later, he was able to talk to her and arrange to steal her and her children away in the dark.

There was great joy when she returned. She later married Pierre Duhamel, who raised her half-Indian children as his own. One of these children was to become Albert Lacombe's grandmother.

For my parents the days on the trail rolled by to the leisured pace of the big team, with every day bringing new interests. A red fox trotted beside the trail one morning. With a loud bark, Brownie jumped from Sam's sleigh to give chase. She was soon back, out-manoeuvered by the fox, but pleased with her brief burst of freedom.

The travellers had been staying at hotels along the route in order to give Mother and Carlton as much rest as possible. Although these stopovers slowed them up considerably, this had not really inconvenienced Sam as he had a heavy load and his team needed the rests. Now, Dad warned Mother, they were leaving civilization behind.

CHAPTER TWO

Mother's Story

My maternal great-grandmother was born Carolyn Bachman in the Low Countries, now known as Holland and Belgium. She was only four when her family was forced to flee their homeland in the midst of revolution. They left behind the chaotic ruins and barricaded streets of a war-torn land, and relocated in the relative stability of Germany. There she was raised and wed to a young German clockmaker. She bore him five sons, the youngest of whom was my grandfather, Walter Valentine Houck.

It was the time of Bismarck and the building of a united and conquering Germany, a Germany that needed young men for her army. To save her sons from conscription, my great-grandmother uprooted the family again. They came to America, to the thriving city of Buffalo, New York, in the mid-1800s. There, my great-grandfather set up again as a clockmaker, on the city's outskirts. The family bought an acre of land with plenty of room for fruit trees and a large garden. Within a few years the city grew up around them.

The quaint house with its hollyhocks to the eaves and masses of morning glories, sweet-williams, and roses in the garden was the beauty spot of the neighbourhood. My great-grandfather, an excellent carpenter, built the house himself and filled it with clocks of every size and description. He set them so their chimes sounded in order, starting with the smallest and most musical, then on to the more strident tones until, finally, to the old grandfather clock that bonged out the hours with great authority. They were a source of amusement to old and young, a free show for whomever dropped in.

My great-grandfather Houck was also an inventor. He developed a machine for making barrel staves and later invented a part for the cotton gin. The profits from these and other inventions, together with his earnings from his clockmaking business, gave the big family a healthy living in their new country.

The family's fifth son, Walter, was born in the United States in 1862 and christened in the Lutheran church his family attended. As a boy he showed a mechanical talent and an inventive curiosity. Since there were few schools teaching mechanics in those days, Walter found work in a bicycle manufacturing shop after he left school. As a young man he belonged to a cycling club that went on jaunts from city to city. Like his father, Walter turned his talents to mechanical inventions and eventually took out patents on several parts for bicycles, motor cars, and airplanes. One of his patents was for the Hartford Hydraulic Shock Absorber, which he sold to an English firm. He claimed he also developed the piston-type shock absorber, now used in aircraft, but that his plans were photographed and stolen. He went on to make other inventions and his reward was a tidy fortune that was to provide well for him until the end of his life.

At the age of twenty-one, Walter met my grandmother, sixteen-year-old Catherine Demmons. She was a child of society, the daughter of a wealthy sculptor, and a Catholic. She and her twin sister were known as the Demmons beauties, and their parents sent to New York for their clothes. Petite, blonde, and blue-eyed with a quick Irish wit and charm, Catherine was expected to take her place with her sister as one of Buffalo's leading debutantes. She was her parents' pride and joy, and they were deeply disappointed when she eloped with my grandfather. Her mother never forgave her. Not only was Walter the son of immigrants, he was a Protestant as well.

The young couple met on a beautiful spring evening when Walter helped his brother deliver a clock to the convent the Demmons sisters attended. My grandmother said it was love at first sight. Walter whispered to her to meet him outside the convent walls, which she did, and she was found innocently picking flowers when he left later. They continued to meet by the convent walls in a clandestine courtship and a few months later they eloped.

Although Walter was earning a good living, Catherine had been raised with servants and did not even know how to make her own bed. It was too much to expect of the young society girl to learn to keep house, to cook, and to care for Eva, the child born to her within the first year of her marriage. To make matters worse, Walter continually compared her to his mother, who was an excellent housekeeper. Catherine began to resent her husband's parents, even though, never having had a daughter, they were anxious to help and welcomed her into their family.

If her own parents had forgiven and supported her, she might have made a go of it. Her father tried, but he became ill of stonecutter consumption and died soon after his first grandchild, Eva, was born. (Many of his works, including the famed Soldier's Monument, still stand in Buffalo.) Although their shared grief brought her and her mother and sister together, they never let Catherine forget she had married beneath her.

My mother was born two years after Eva, in the year 1888, and was named Olive. She was her father's favourite and always turned to him for comfort and understanding. When we were children, Mother often told us of the day just after she turned four when her father came home full of excitement and announced to his daughters they had twin baby brothers, one for each of them to play with. Picking both girls up, he danced them into the parlour. Mother burst into tears saying she wanted to be his baby, and he comforted her telling her she would always be his baby girl.

My tiny, five-foot-tall grandmother was now glad to welcome the husky Irish girl Walter hired to help cope with the children, who had suddenly doubled in number. Grandmother was so occupied getting through her days and nights that she no longer complained about her husband's involvement with his cycling friends.

One day, four years later, Walter came home and insisted his wife go out with his cycling group – they had something important to discuss and wanted her cooperation. There was to be a big race, and Walter wanted to make a little bike for each of the four-year-old boys, so they could ride around the track as a grandstand attraction. Children's bicycles were not manufactured in those days, and Walter worked very hard making the two little racing machines, using large dinner plates as patterns for the wheels. All the family helped the boys learn to ride. I have a photo of the boys, looking a little frightened, all alone on the big track with a huge crowd watching from the grandstand. The applause was deafening, for the twins as well as for Walter, a very popular racer.

I wish I could say this family lived happily ever after, but this was not the case. Less than a month after the race, Walter left my grandmother for another woman and took the boys with him. Catherine sold her house and used all the money searching for them. Two years after her husband and sons disappeared, Catherine heard he was living in another city and travelled to it by train. She was walking past a house there, when through a window she saw two small boys playing. When no one answered the doorbell, she broke a window and jumped into the house, only to find she had been mistaken. Catherine never saw her sons again.

Grandmother became convinced the strong brotherhood of the Masonic Lodge, to which her husband belonged, was protecting him. To support herself and her children she had to find a job. She had no training but was able to obtain work as a clerk in Macy's Department Store. However, she found it too difficult to cope with two children and a job.

Olive was sent to live with a distant cousin of her father's, a woman she called Aunt Em. Aunt Em, her husband Walter Sherman, an engineer on a Lake Erie tug boat, and Aunt Em's sister, Carrie, became my mother's new family. Words can not describe the happiness the eight-year-old girl brought to this childless couple. A beautiful woman who loved my mother as if she had been her own, Aunt Em instilled in the child a great faith that would never leave her. She also taught her always to tell the absolute truth. Mother could be easy-going and lenient with her own children, but, like Aunt Em, she always insisted on the truth.

My grandmother was left to cope with a job and with Eva, who had always been hard to manage. Now, without her father's firm hand, Eva was even more difficult. Thankful that my mother was being looked after, Catherine tried to put the past behind. Still in her twenties, she was more beautiful than ever, but she never remarried. She seldom visited her younger daughter, perhaps realizing she was happy and involved in her new home.

A family by the name of Freeland had recently moved to Buffalo, to the same street as Aunt Em. Their youngest daughter, Bertha, met Olive at church and the two little girls became fast friends. Mrs. Freeland's heart went out to little Olive and she was included in the family circle as often as possible.

The years sped by and the happy child became a well-adjusted young woman. At sixteen and a half Olive attained the same height as her mother, but still hoped to stretch another inch or two. Her steady blue eyes were widespaced in a heart-shaped face, their brightness contrasting with the olive skin she inherited from her Belgian ancestors. Aunt Em, fearing such a pretty girl would become vain, made her pull her long fair hair back from her face and secure it with a large bow. However, this arrangement suited my mother's delicate features, showing off her perfect widow's peak. The severity of the style was softened by small tendrils that curled around her face and the nape of her neck.

Walter and Em Sherman and their little Ollie spent many hours selecting a teaching college she would attend the year after she finished high school. It was a terrible shock to them when Catherine arrived one day and insisted Olive come home with her and get a job; Eva had lost hers again and someone had to help pay the bills. Neither Aunt Em's pleas nor my mother's tears could change her mind. She did, however, give them time to get used to the idea.

This was another difficult period in my mother's life, and it left her with a resentment toward my grandmother which she never quite overcame. She had accepted her Aunt Em and Uncle Walter as her parents; they had given her the security she needed to heal the scars caused by the loss of her father and brothers, and she returned their love as generously as they gave it. Her mother, recognizing this strong bond and regretting her neglect, had the wisdom to give them a little longer time together. Aunt Em hid her own sorrow and soon had Olive believing that working in a big store could be an education as well as an adventure. Aunt Em's sense of fairness made her realize how fortunate they had been to have had Mother for eight years of her life.

Shortly after starting to work for Macy's, Olive found herself surrounded with many new friends who, like herself, were working to help their families. They were a fun-loving group, and she soon overcame her shyness and became more outgoing. There were advantages to working for a big store, including boating excursions on Lake Erie, dances, and other planned outings. But she remained close to her aunt and uncle, spending many Sundays with them, and continued to visit next door at the Freelands with her friend, Bertha.

CHAPTER THREE

Bunkhouse Warnings

Although darkness lay all around him, Dad instinctively knew morning had come. Pulling on his pants and shirt, he groped for his heavy socks and boots, then felt his way to the cookstove where he found the kindling and a few pinecones they had picked up along the trail. In a few minutes a fire was blazing, its cheery glow creating a small pool of warm brightness.

The bunkhouse where they had spent the night was little more than a log shack, sparsely furnished with wooden bunks along the wall, a small table, and an ancient cookstove. Yet, during a week on the trail, they learned to be grateful for such lodgings, built by farmers and traders as accommodation for any traveller who could afford the going rate of sixty cents per night.

The night had been cold. Dad had to break through a layer of ice before he could fill the kettle from the water bucket. Glancing over at his wife and child, he decided to let them sleep a few extra minutes while he attended to the horses. Outside it was cold and clear, the stars hanging like glittering diamonds against the darkness of the sky, and his heavy boots crunched on new-fallen snow. Babe and Girlie whinnied a welcome from their stalls. They had been given a good feed of oats and hay the night before and were soon watered and harnessed and ready to go.

The sun would not rise above the hills for another two hours on this cold February morning, but a grey dawn was beginning to lighten the eastern sky as Dad approached the bunkhouse. The smoke from his fire drifted back on the frosty air. Its pungent scent reminded him of his younger days around campfires in faraway Africa.

He lit the coal oil lamp, then gently woke his wife. She stirred and reluctantly opened her eyes; her face was drawn and weary. She was young, and he knew the past weeks had been hard on her, especially as she had had to cope with an active eighteen-month-old child, fretful from teething. Yet she never complained, and Dad thought guiltily that he could have been more patient. But he had been a bachelor for years, and old habits were hard to break at the age of thirty-four.

Shivering, Mother stepped onto the cold floor. Her sleep had been disturbed by other outfits pulling into the yard during the night; for hours she had tossed and turned on the hard wooden bunk, its only mattress the quilt she had folded under the rough blankets. Then she had remembered the advice of her Aunt Em, and she prayed for the courage and strength to endure what lay ahead. Her heart lighter, she had then been able to sink into a sound sleep.

Mother dressed hurriedly in a skirt and blouse over several petticoats, put on long black stockings, and heavy shoes. Because she was pregnant, she was spared the agony of corsets, then considered de rigueur for every woman, no matter what her living conditions. After washing in a grimy basin, she prepared breakfast, then quickly changed and dressed the child half under the bed-clothes, while he whimpered and tried to crawl back into his warm nest.

Half an hour later, the sleigh was packed and they were ready for another long day on the trail. As they pulled out of the yard, mother and baby cuddled under the quilts against the chill wind. Carlton was beginning to fret, his mouth feverish from the teeth he was cutting. To make matters worse, they had lost his bottle for water. Mother rocked him back and forth, soothing him to sleep. Dad had promised that they would be having lunch at a stopping-off place noted for its excellent cooking. It was popular with most travellers, though, and unless they arrived in good time they might miss out on their meal.

Within an hour the sun had climbed halfway up the sky, not shedding much warmth yet, but causing a sparkling on the crisp snow. An hour later they heard the jingle of harnesses and, looking back, saw Sam's rig approaching at a brisk pace. Mother and Dad laughed at Brownie proudly perched on the seat beside Sam, "Looking," according to Mother, "for all the world like a princess being driven through the streets of her capital by her coachman."

They reached the stopping place later than they expected. The steep icy hills had made it necessary to chain-lock the sleigh runners in order to get safely down, slowing their progress. The farmer's wife met them at the door and noticed Mother's tired face. She led her into a bedroom for a rest while lunch was being prepared. Mother sank down on the soft bed and fell sound asleep. Half an hour later she awoke to find the young daughter had left hot water, soap, and towels. Wryly amused, she wondered if she looked as grubby as she felt. While lathering her face, neck, and arms with the scented soap, she decided that she liked the direct, straightforward manner of these northerners who reached out to help one another.

As she brushed her long, shiny hair in front of the mirror, Mother was pleased to note that days in the fresh air and sunshine had added an attractive glow to her complexion. She chided herself for vanity, yet the look of appreciation on the faces of the men when she entered the dining room did more for her morale than the excellent meal. Dad was seated beside Sam with Carlton on his knee, but seeing Mother enter the room came forward, happy to claim the pretty young woman. Mother, flushing slightly, was relieved when their hostess beckoned them to be seated. As their eyes met, the two women exchanged a conspiratorial smile. Only women who have been through a pregnancy can know how important it is to look their best.

Dad introduced Mother to a freighter whom he knew from earlier days on the trail. Several men were struggling into heavy coonskin- and sheepskin-lined coats preparing to leave. Dad's friend explained to Mother that they were freighters on their way to Edmonton to pick up provisions to be hauled to Grouard and that the trek across Lesser Slave Lake was the worst part of the trip. Dad was listening now. Howling winds sweeping across this unprotected area could freeze a person's face, hands, or feet, if the utmost precaution were not taken. Freighters who could afford it bought fur coats or sheepskin-lined ones. Mother was thankful they had coats with large fur collars to protect their faces. Looking at her feet, the man told Mother she would never make it if she had to walk any distance during a storm in the shoes she was wearing. He advised her and Dad to buy Indian moccasins and moccasin rubbers along with heavy knee-length socks. He went on to tell them that when his own wife came out with him, she wore a pair of men's heavy macinaw pants under her long skirt in the worst weather.

"But surely," Mother said anxiously, "the weather won't be that severe by the end of March or first of April." Seeing her concern, he hastened to apologize, saying he had not meant to frighten her, but often the worst storms occurred in March and April.

The next morning as they waved goodbye to their hosts, Mother marvelled at the hospitality and kindness they had experienced from families along the route. Life for these pioneers, she knew, was not easy, especially for the women who had to cope with everyday household chores and raising a family. As well, they helped their husbands bring in much-needed extra cash by opening their homes to travellers. Yet they were always ready to offer a warm welcome and cheery words of advice to those who came to their doors as strangers.

The farm they were leaving was located at the foot of a steep hill and Dad noted with relief that the other rigs had made it safely to the top. Sam took the lead, urging his team on, ready to jump out and inset a steel contraption, called a "dog," under the runners if the sleigh started to slip backward. Then it was Babe's and Girlie's turn, and the sturdy Clydesdales plodded steadily up the hill. Mother was ready to take the reins if Dad should find it necessary to use the dog. She had driven the sleigh quite often on the straight-of-way and had such faith in the dependable performance of the team she felt sure they would make it to the top with no trouble.

When the going was easy, Dad sometimes let Carlton sit on his knee and hold the reins, and the little boy would urge the horses to "giddyup" in imitation of his father. Now Carlton stood, holding onto the front of the sleigh, absorbed in the excitement and success of surmounting the steep hill.

The day had become unseasonably warm and the air was heady with perfume from the swelling poplar buds. Cheeky blue jays followed them hoping for a handout, and Mother caught sight of a red-capped woodpecker drumming industriously on a hollow log. The sky curved overhead in a wide blue arc. Mother's heart filled with joy as she realized she was participating in a great adventure. She would not have missed it for all the soft living offered by the biggest city.

As they travelled, Dad could not help comparing this northern land with South Africa, the country that had claimed so many years of his life. He began speaking to Mother now of the sun-washed plains, carved with great furrows cut by steep dry-water beds and dotted with dark-green camelthorn trees, in whose branches hung the enormous communal nest of thousands of dryland weaver birds – each new generation adding to the nest until it reached the size of a haystack, finally snapping off the sturdy branch that supported it.

CHAPTER FOUR

My Father's Story

My father was born John Wilbur Freeland in Mowequa, Illinois, in the year 1876. He was the eldest of seven children, two girls and five boys. His family traced its roots to England's Reformation era, when an early Freeland was reputed to have saved the life of Oliver Cromwell while serving as an officer in his army. Freeland was rewarded with an estate and the naming of a village after him. (In 1960 my husband Ged and I travelled to England as guests of the Commonwealth. We were treated royally and, while returning to London after visiting the theatre at Stratford-on-Avon, we passed through the Village of Freeland.)

My grandfather, Charles Wesley Freeland, was a good farmer, providing well for his large family. But after he died, financial troubles began to pile up, and when Dad turned eighteen it was decided he would leave home in the fall to try to find some means to improve his family's situation. He worked hard helping bring in the harvest, and then the time came to leave. Saying goodbye, especially to his mother, was a painful experience. They had no way of knowing when they would be together again. She looked with pride at her fine-looking son, with his fair complexion, brown eyes, and flashing smile. Although not very tall, he carried his slim, athletic body well. She knew he was adventuresome – and that the world is wide. With very little money in his pocket and a few articles of clothing in a pack on his back, he set out for New York, promising to send money as soon as he could.

Although impressed with New York, Dad decided he could do better in the Old World. He met a couple of sailors who informed him their ship, a freighter, was sailing for England in a few days. He managed to get aboard and hide under a tarp in a lifeboat, where, he told us later, he nearly suffocated. When the boat was well out to sea, he went to the captain, admitted he was a stowaway, and asked if he could work for his passage.

The ship steamed into Liverpool on a raw, foggy morning. The captain, pleased with Dad's work, asked him to stay on. Dad declined, although he agreed to help unload the cargo so he could earn a few pounds. He then set off for London on foot, sleeping at pubs, eating his frugal meals alongside motley crews whose strange accents intrigued him. He listened to them gripe about wages and conditions, much as men did at home.

The youthful adventurer would always remember the thrill of seeing London for the first time. It was a city of such antiquity, this young farm boy could only look at it with reverence. He vowed someday he would return with enough money to enjoy its pleasures.

The jobs available to a boy of his age and experience paid him hardly enough to support himself, so he decided to seek his fortune further afield. After seeing a sign advertising work for young men in South Africa's diamond mines, he once again set out on foot – back to Liverpool. There he was able to find a berth aboard a ship headed for Cape Town.

Cape Town was then a beautiful city and has an almost-perfect climate. But Kimberley, where the diamond mines are located, was a raw and rowdy boomtown. In later years, Dad used to tell us harrowing tales of the punishment handed out to tribesmen who tried to steal diamonds while working in the mines. A favourite penalty for theft was to cut a path in the thief's flesh and insert the diamond in the wound. The men were kept down in the mines for two to three weeks at a stretch, thus giving the cuts time to heal over, sealing the rough stone within. A few of the precious stones were successfully stolen, but usually the thieves were caught during thorough searches upon surfacing. In those days, the mine owners in that raw country made their own laws, and punishment meted out to the poor devils was terrible. Some were dragged to the woods where a couple of rough characters, hired for the purpose, beat them to a bloody pulp with a *sjambid*, a whip of cured rhinoceros hide. In some cases, thieves were actually put to death.

The tribesmen who worked in the mines were usually young Kaffirs or Zulus, some them of sons of chiefs. The pay was only a few shillings a week, but they coveted the guns given to men who worked out a three-year term. Natives were valuable miners, as only black men would endure the terrible conditions in the diggings while working for such low pay. These tribesmen were raised within the strict structure of highly-disciplined family life in their *kraals*, beginning at puberty to train for the fighting regiments. Stealing was against their law except when it concerned their enemies, and the white man was considered an enemy as the Boers often apprehended young men on their way to the mines and forced them to work on the land. As my father became aware of this situation, he felt torn between loyalty to his employers and sympathy for the young tribesmen. Dad was honest and not afraid of hard work and was soon given a promotion, which brought him into closer contact with the natives. As he made friends with them, he was able to learn their language, and once they began to trust him, was able to persuade many of them to give up their thieving practices.

It was about this time that he made friends with Frederick Jones, a young Englishman with an interest in horse racing – an interest my father began to share. Both men acquired strong, sturdy racing animals. Dad named his Stars and Stripes. After Dad's death, we found among his possessions a small blue booklet listing him as the owner of Stars and Stripes, one of the horses who ran in Kimberley's first Cantata.

Dad made good use of Stars and Stripes as he and Frederick spent their holidays travelling across the countryside on horseback, sometimes hundreds of miles, often staying at the family *kraals* of the young men he had helped at the mines. He told us how vulnerable the two of them felt the first time they approached a Zulu settlement.

Each *kraal* had around it a stockade to guard against predators and marauders. These settlements of beehive-shaped huts were guarded by naked little boys who, on sighting the strangers, dashed off to alert the *kraal*. This brought out the women, naked from the waist up, balancing hollow gourds on their heads – an exercise that give them a stately dignity of bearing. My father and his friend found themselves looking into the inky eyes of these astonished women. After my father assured them that they came in peace and brought news of their kinsmen, they were taken to the settlement's stronghold. Warriors streamed from the huts and formed a line on either side of Dad and Frederick in deadly stillness; with the inscrutable gaze of a lion measuring it's prey before beginning to stalk, each watched the two white men. Neither Frederick nor Dad looked from right to left as they passed through the menacing ranks.

The chief, alerted that two white men with news of their kinsmen were approaching, came forward to meet them. Having been briefed on Zulu salutations and behaviour, the two conducted themselves appropriately. In return, they were welcomed and refreshed with millet beer and delicious corn and honey cakes.

In private, the chief asked Dad if he would take back a message to his son. It was of such poetic beauty that my father never forgot it. Standing, they looked into each other's eyes, hands clasped in friendship, while the chief said, "Stay in peace my son, and may the days melt like mist above the desert sand, until we smile each upon the other." My Dad repeated the message to the chief, whose eyes glistened as he accepted this stranger's role in the lives of their young men.

A feast was prepared that night in honour of Dad and Frederick and the tribe rejoiced in the news of their sons. It was followed by a tribal dance. The part Dad liked best came after the men had grown weary of sprinting and thrusting the *assegai*. They squatted around the fires and a single voice started a battle song. Others joined. Soon the veldt for miles around echoed to the deep melodious sound of their singing. After listening to the oft-repeated words, Dad and Frederick joined in. Before leaving the next morning, they distributed presents of salt—which the Zulus craved – beads, and other trinkets, and received an invitation to return.

The two young men found their way to many such settlements and, over the years, became fluent in many dialects. At the outbreak of the Boer War, their knowledge of the territory enabled them to enlist as scouts for Queen Victoria. They were kept on the move with assignments among the tribesmen, many of whom were already friends. After the war, Frederick and Dad were both presented with silver cigarette boxes engraved with the Queen's initials, for outstanding service. Dad treasured his box which I was later to inherit.

The natives never quite knew what to make of these two laughing young men; the tribesmen believed a serious and dignified countenance was more becoming to men, and levity was only for women and children.

Shortly before their marriage, Mother asked Dad how he knew when he had won over a native chief, he replied, "Why, when he offered us one of his wives for the night, of course." Dad was soon to regret his teasing. She stoutly refused to return to South Africa with him, saying it was not a fit place to raise a family. Although she would never admit it, Dad suspected she was really afraid she might run into one of his off-spring there.

Dad had saved his soldier's salary, and was able to open a butcher shop and start a few smaller enterprises in Kimberley, hiring natives to help run them. His big break came a few years later when tsetse flies caused the outbreak of a disease among cattle in the Kimberley area. Whole herds died. Dad and Frederick and several native employees rode hundreds of miles into the outlying countryside to buy large numbers of cattle at reasonable prices and herd them back to Kimberley. They made a small fortune from this venture.

After fourteen years in South Africa it was time to go home, but Dad decided to travel and see more of the world on his way. There was a powerful difference between viewing the English coastline from the first-class deck of a luxury liner and viewing it from the railing of the cattle boat on which he had worked his way to Africa. He fulfilled his dream and had a wonderful time in London with Frederick, taking in the shows, staying in the best hotels, even singing in an amateur show. He then toured the continent in style before booking passage back to the United States.

Mother arrived at the Freeland home one particular Sunday to find the family in a state of excitement. They had just received news that Wilbur, the oldest son, was coming home. Mother had shared news of the adventures of Bertha's brother, whose generosity had made it possible for the family to relocate to Buffalo. When she was younger, she had pretended to be a bit bored when her friend bragged about him. Now she was as excited as the family. She even bought a pretty new dress for his homecoming party.

Meanwhile, Dad had been hearing about pretty Olive Houck from his younger brother, Edlow, and reading between the lines, realized Edlow would like to be more than just friends with her. Dad was right. Edlow had fallen for Olive and they had been seeing quite a bit of each other. Edlow was taking a special course that summer at a school close to Macy's where she worked. He often took her to lunch, but my thrifty Mother was soon packing lunches which they shared in a nearby park. The day finally came when Edlow looked into her eyes and realized he was in love, but he also knew Olive regarded him only as a dear friend.

It was after Bertha sent Dad a picture of herself and Ollie, that he decided to go home. Frederick tried to talk him out of it, but Dad said he had neglected his mother long enough. He planned on returning to Africa though, after along visit. He then showed his friend Mother's picture, admitting he was perhaps foolish in hoping this lovely young woman would marry him, but he was going to try and win her.

The big steamship moved slowly into New York harbour. Dad stood at the rail among the other passengers, all of them silent as they gazed at the city just coming into view. The silver sky was filled with dark puffy clouds and a damp mist sprayed the ship. Some of that mist seemed to get into Dad's eyes as he caught sight of the Statue of Liberty silhouetted against the early morning sky. This was the sight he had been waiting for, the sight that told him that, after fourteen years, he was home.

His mother shed a few tears at their reunion, and there was great rejoicing in the Freeland home. Dad brought them all beautiful gifts, but he kept two gems. He later had them set into rings for Mother. One was an emerald which Dad had a jeweller place in a setting surrounded by diamonds. The other was a blood-red ruby that Mother wore for many years and then gave to me since it is my birthstone.

The Freelands planned a large lawn party in honour of Wilbur, and hoped for good weather. Olive was a bit late in arriving, but faithful Edlow was waiting for her at the station in his buggy. Dad caught his first glimpse of her as she stepped gracefully down from the buggy, completely unaware that he was watching her from behind a tree. He thought she looked lovely in her new flower-sprigged white gown and noticed how the breeze caught the filmy material outlining her petite figure. A matching parasol framed her face as she laughed up at Edlow. Dad smiled to himself, thinking that her picture had not done her justice.

He stepped forward to meet her, and Edlow, a bit startled, asked what the honoured guest was doing here. Dad was hardly aware of his brother; he had eyes only for the lovely girl. Dad told her later that from that first moment he was a "gonner." It was not just Dad's heart that began beating in double time. Mother was equally affected. Edlow decided he had better put a stop to the shared looks of admiration and introduced them. Mother was surprised by Dad's English accent, but he explained he had lived and worked with Englishmen for many years, and speaking as they did made him more acceptable to them. He assured her it would soon wear off.

His family came to claim him, anxious to introduce the world traveller to their friends. Mother was glad to be alone for a moment, hoping to shake off an odd premonition, a sudden glimpse into the future, warning her this was the man she would marry. Shaken, she joined her friends. When Aunt Em and Uncle Walter left early, she went with them, but agreed to join the Freelands for a picnic the next day.

Over the next few weeks my parents became more and more absorbed in each other. Although their lives had been very different, both had characters molded by very special people – his mother and her Aunt Em – giving them many similar characteristics.

Unfortunately, Grandmother Freeland's health was not good and Dad became increasingly concerned. She had arthritis which the cold damp winds whipping off the Great Lakes aggravated. With some of the money he had earned in Africa he hoped to buy a home in California and establish his family there. They agreed, and a few months later he took them to Bakersfield and helped them find a house large enough for them all. His mother tried to persuade him to buy a business and settle there. Although he helped his brothers financially so they could buy a hotel, he did not feel California was the place for him.

By now, mother was wearing Dad's ring and was happily preparing her trousseau with the help of her mother and aunts. The only blight on the engagement was that Mother refused to go to Africa. Because of her broken home she had a great need for a family, and she did not think a "heathen" country like Africa was a good place to raise children. This disturbed my father. He had been very happy in South Africa and wanted to return. But he was learning that this amiable Dutch-Irish girl, twelve years his junior, could be very stubborn. He decided to give up Africa and keep Mother. When he asked if she would go west with him, she agreed, and he left for Omaha, Nebraska, to look at a movie theatre that was for sale.

It was a shock for Mother to receive a letter from Wilbur telling her he had bought the theatre, and asking her to join him in Omaha, where they would be married. He explained he was trying to learn as much about the business as possible before the former owners left. He was lonely and a little worried about his transaction and hoped she would join him soon. He had even found a Methodist clergyman, who agreed to marry them. After reading and re-reading his letter, Mother came to the conclusion that he was really very shy under his confident manner and had been dreading the big wedding.

Although she was almost as disappointed as her relatives and friends, Mother agreed. She added some warm practical clothes to her trousseau, and a few days later she was saying goodbye to her family and friends who had come to see her off at the railway station. Edlow, who would soon be joining his family in California, and who had been avoiding Mother since Wilbur's homecoming party, was suddenly his old teasing self again. He gave her his blessings, telling her jokingly that he would be waiting if she ever got tired of his older brother. They all laughed, but Mother shed a few tears. She had already said goodbye to her mother and Eva. Aunt Em, however, would not let the parting be a sad one. She handed mother a large bouquet of roses as the others pelted her with confetti. The conductor yelled, "All aboard!" Edlow helped her up the steps, and she was off.

It was the first time Mother had travelled more than a few miles outside Buffalo. It was early November, and the day was clear and bright; a few coloured leaves still clung to the trees. Just a few hundred yards from the track Mother spotted a farm, and she watched as the farmer drove his cattle home with the help of his son and a dog. She was thrilled. She had never seen a farm before, or real farm animals.

After several days of travelling, Mother was beginning to wonder if the man she was journeying so many miles to marry was just a dream. The next morning the porter handed her a telegram. It was from Dad saying he was counting the days until she arrived and would be waiting for her at the Omaha station. He signed it, "With all my love, Wilbur." It had come at just the right time and made the sun shine again for Mother.

In Omaha, the clergyman and his wife insisted that Mother be their guest for the night. They ordered her to rest after the long trip, and reminded Dad it was considered bad luck for the groom to see his bride before the ceremony in the morning.

The wedding was a simple but pretty. Dad had ordered flowers and hired an organist and soloist, a friend of the clergyman, who sang "Oh Promise Me."

The young couple found a furnished apartment, deciding to wait until spring before looking for a more permanent residence. The days were still bright and sunny, giving them a chance to explore the countryside and drive with horse and buggy along the Missouri River. Although the trees were bare of leaves, bright autumn flowers – goldenrod and blue gentian – still bloomed along the roadway. Weekends often found them at the big farmers' market where mother loved to shop. They always went early so they could watch from the buggy as eggs, poultry, butter, and vegetables were loaded onto the stalls. Mother made friends with one of the farmer's children, a freckled-faced boy of ten, who helped her forget her homesickness.

Dad had taken over the management of the theatre but was starting to worry about his business. The former owner had hinted he strongly suspected some of the profits were slipping into the wrong pockets. The projectionist was married to the cashier, which added to their difficulties. They soon discovered why Dad was able to buy the business at such a good price. A new theatre was due to open shortly in the same district. Although Mother wondered why Dad had not checked this out before buying, she held her tongue.

Mother would not tolerate being cheated though and, in view of the drop in sales, came to an understanding with their employees that she would take over in the ticket booth. Dad was not happy about his wife working, but Mother enjoyed going to the theatre with him everyday. It got her out of cooking and, as she laughingly told him, she got to see the shows free.

It was not long before Mother discovered that she was pregnant. She was thrilled, but hugged her secret to her heart for a week before she told Dad, afraid the news might add to his worries. She was unprepared for his happiness at the prospect of becoming a father.

He decided to sell the theatre and was able to find a buyer, although he took a considerable loss. Northern Canada had been much in the news lately and Dad had become intrigued by this new land of opportunity. In 1911, once again Mother found herself on the move, this time to Edmonton, Alberta, where my father bought a hotel and where, the following August, my brother Carlton was born.

Business was good and Dad intended to buy land near Edmonton. But he was beginning to feel restless. He was used to an outdoor life and the businesses he'd been involved in were no challenge. Leaving his young wife to manage the hotel, he became a freighter, joining that hardy breed who hauled supplies by horse and sled to communities along the Athabasca Trail between Edmonton and Athabasca Landing.

Many of the hotel guests were men who stayed only long enough to buy supplies and arrange transportation further north, lured by the prospects of homesteading good land. So Mother was not particularly surprised when Dad came home one day and announced that they, too, were heading north, to the new but quickly-growing town of Grouard, where he had bought another hotel.

CHAPTER FIVE

Tales Along the Trail

Dad turned to Mother, noticing how relaxed she looked as she basked in the warm sun with Carlton snuggled beside her. He said, "I hope you realize, Ollie, this warm spell won't last. It could be bitterly cold tomorrow."

"Really Wilbur," she replied, "have you forgotten that I've spent two long winters here. I've been told many times, 'Spring can't be counted on until the Canada geese can be heard winging to their nesting grounds.'"

Their conversation turned to Edmonton and the newspaper article that first drew their attention to the city. It was hard to believe that only twenty-three years ago the thriving, bustling city they had just left behind was a small village of less than five hundred people. The article had revealed that a century ago Angus Shaw made his way up the Saskatchewan River to build the fur trading post of Fort Augustus, later to become Fort Edmonton. He so liked the new land that he wrote describing it as a rich country, endowed with a variety of wildlife.

The land proved to be fertile, producing crops that brought settlers from all over the world. Coal was discovered nearby and, only forty-six years after my parents' arrival, the first Leduc oil well blew in. Many overlanders, stopping at Edmonton for supplies on their way to the Klondike, heard of the hardships of other goldseekers farther along the trail and in the fields and decided to stay where they were. Their ranks were swollen by disappointed prospectors who managed to make it back. Some of them made a good living panning gold along the Saskatchewan River. Among the most famous was Tom Clover, who made a sizeable strike on a sandbar before settling on land near Edmonton. Clover Bar was named for him.

Edmonton was favourably situated for the fur trade. It could be reached by boat or over the Red River cart trails that wound across the prairies and through the bushland from Fort Gary, now Winnipeg. The arrival of the railroad also increased the number of settlers to the area.

When Mother told us of her first impressions of Edmonton, she said it was the old Hudson's Bay fort that caught her attention. The palisade around the fort was 300 feet long, 200 feet wide, with a height of 20 feet. It had the usual sentinels and was equipped with bastions and old iron cannons, giving it a look of strength and stability. It was necessary to enclose the lot in a strong stockade. The Cree claimed this as their territory and erected lodges along the creeks and rivers between Edmonton and the Athabasca river, and were constantly at war with the Plains Indians. When the two tribes met at the fort to trade their furs, bitter fighting erupted from time to time. It is not certain if the cannons at the fort were ever fired in anger, but my parents were told that one exploded during the New Year's festivities of 1852, killing the blacksmith who set it off.

Chief Factor John Rowand's residence, built within the palisade in 1825, was the most pretentious habitation west of Fort Gary because of its great size and real glass windows. Jokingly referred to as Rowand's Folly, it was, however, put to good use. Besides a great dining room with many fireplaces that were never allowed to go out, the building contained a hall used mainly for the dances that followed the dinners and feasts expected of the company's chief factor. An old timer who had served as a company guide, told my parents he remembered well the delicious food that was served in those days.

Paul Kane, an artist and author, wrote in his book, *Wanderings of an Artist Among the Indians of North America*

(Edmonton: Hurtig, 1968) of such a feast he attended in 1847.

On Christmas Day the flag was hoisted, and all
appeared in their best and gaudiest style, to do
honour to the holiday.... About two o'clock,
we sat down to dinner. Our party consisted of
Mr. Harriett, the chief, and three clerks, Mr.
Thebo, the Roman Catholic missionary from
Manitou Lake [St Anne] about thirty miles off,
Mr. Rundell, the Wesleyan missionary, who
resided within the pickets and myself.... The
dining-hall, probably the largest room in the
fort, was about fifty by twenty-five feet, well
warmed by large fires, which are scarcely ever
allowed to go out. The walls and ceilings are
boarded.... These boards are painted in a style
of the most startling barbaric gaudiness, and the
ceiling filled with centre-pieces of fantastic gilt
scrolls, making altogether a saloon which no
white man would enter for the first time
without a start, and which the Indians always
looked upon with awe and wonder....
No tablecloth shed its snowy whiteness over the
board; no silver candelabra or gaudy china
interfered with its simple magnificence. The
bright tin plates and dishes reflected jolly faces
and burnished gold can give no truer zest to a
feast....
   At the head ...was a large dish of boiled
buffalo-hump; at the foot smoked a boiled calf.
Start not, gentle reader, the calf is very small,
and is taken from the cow by a Caesarean
operation long before it attains its full growth.
This, boiled whole, is one of the most esteemed
dishes amongst the epicures of the interior. My
pleasing duty was to help dish the mouffle, or
dried moose nose; the gentleman on my left

distributed, with graceful impartiality, the white
fish, delicately browned in buffalo marrow. The
worthy priest helped with the buffalo tongue,
whilst Mr. Rundell cut up the beavers' tails.
Nor was the other gentleman left unemployed,
as all his spare time was occupied in dissecting a
roast wild goose. The centre of the table was
graced with piles of potatoes, turnips, and bread
conveniently placed, so that each could help
himself without interrupting the labours of his
companions. Such was our jolly Christmas
dinner at Edmonton and long will it remain in
my memory, although no pies, or puddings, or
blanc manges, shed their fragrance over the
scene. [pp. 262-263]

The dance that followed with both Indians and whites,
continued until midnight, when everyone was exhausted. And
so with feasting and dancing and good cheer, the prairie elite at
Edmonton sped another Christmas into eternity.

● ● ●

The first links between the Saskatchewan River and the
elbow of the Athabasca were the trails of the Kristenaux, or
Cree. Since 1794, they had been bringing their furs over the
same routes to the trading post at Edmonton House. There,
trails originated at the mouths of the Sturgeon and Terre
Blanche, or White Earth, rivers, near present-day Pakan. It was
along these winding trails that the natives of the woods dragged
their *wickiups* each year, on their way to the plains for their
buffalo hunt.

Some trails, such as the one fur-trader Simpson caused to be
hacked out from Fort Assiniboine to Fort Edmonton,
disappeared at the end of the fur trade era, as they were built
especially for fur traders who preferred to keep settlers out.
This was not the case of the Athabasca Trail, which was used by
the traders to bring in supplies and horses to Fort Chipewyan,

Fort Vermillion, St. Mary's by the Peace River, Fort Dunvegan, and Lesser Slave Lake.

In 1848, a Hudson's Bay post was built at Athabasca Landing. The Company took the responsibility of upgrading the Athabasca Trail, building bridges, and operating scows on the Sturgeon, Redwater, and Tawatinaw Rivers. Other improvements were made from time to time, but the trail still skirted sloughs and muskeg and wound around stumps and over corduroy (logs laid side-by-side across the road).

Originally, the trail had started somewhere in the vicinity of Edmonton's 97th, or 99th Streets on the banks high above the Saskatchewan River, near the present site of the MacDonald Hotel. At the time, Edmonton was a small village no more than three or four blocks long and three blocks wide. Located in a clearing, it was hemmed in by forests so dense that, during the 1885 Rebellion, the size of the clearing was doubled around it to give the defenders a chance to observe attacking Indians. The village then consisted of blacksmith shops, a couple of dozen livery stables, a few hotels and the homes of the inhabitants. There were also the larger establishments of the fur traders – the Hudson's Bay, Revillion Frères, J.E. Cornwall, McDougall and Secord, and Johnson and Walker, to name a few. Close to these were other businesses, some of which saw more activity after sundown.

Three trails – the Athabasca, Victoria, and Fort Saskatchewan – merged where they crossed Norwood Boulevard and continued as one until Rat Creek. Here, one branched northwest as the Victoria Trail. Another branch continued on past Belmont and Horse Hills to Sturgeon River, where it definitely became the Athabasca Trail, turning northwest and following the river to its elbow, where it crossed the bridge at the present town of Gibbons. There were other routes out of the city at the time of my parents' departure, but they chose the Athabasca Trail.

Carlton was settling down and becoming a good traveller. Mother smiled as she watched him clutching the end of the reins in his small mittened hands and calling "giddyup" to Babe and

Girlie, helping his father urge the team up a steep slope.

Entranced by the scenery as they made their way along the north shore of a small lake, Mother turned to Dad, and asked, "Does it have a name?" "It's called Lilly Lake," he replied. As she gazed down from a hilltop, she said, "With it's covering of snow, and ringed with dwarf tamarack and spruce, it looks like a pearl." She laughed, when a few miles up the road, Dad pointed out an innocent-looking little stream, saying, "It's called Whiskey Creek. Near here, two enterprising men built a still, turning it's pure water into Athabasca Dew."

They grew tired and hungry as the morning wore on and looked forward to a good lunch at Joe Patry's place. Originally known as Waugh's House it was one of the first stopping houses along the route. Joe's wife had been a Waugh before her marriage, and it was then run by her family. Mother enjoyed hearing the stories, told over lunch, of the early days when buffalo were hunted south of Edmonton.

After the good food and a short rest, my parents followed a little creek until it joined Redwater River (from there it made its way through the Vermillion hills to Half-Way Lake). Although they had three choices of stopping houses, they decided to stop at Eggie's place, Half-Way House, which was the farthest down the line and considered to be half-way to the Landing. It was a hard choice, for Captain Gullion's place was also a favourite with travellers who enjoyed hearing of the feud that had been going on for years between "Jack the Ripper" and Colin Gullion.

Captain Gullion had earned his title as he had been a captain of a boat, the *Peace River*, and had also served as first mate on the *Grahame*. A Scottish immigrant, this man was known throughout the Peace River district for his great wit. He was also considered quite a talker. Jack was a freighter who usually managed to swipe feed for his team whenever he stopped at the Captain's place. In his book *Land of Twelve Foot Davis*, James B. MacGregor, tells this amusing tale:

> Bales of hay he could not resist. Sheaves of
> oats were a challenge to his skill. Guillion's oat

field, half a mile north of the pine bush, was a
sore temptation to him. It became an obsession
with him to outwit Colin Gullion, and many
times he did so. Once, as he was sneaking out
of the hayfield with a bale of hay on his
shoulders, Captain Gullion stole up to him and
quietly set fire to the bale. Jack's expletives and
Gullion's laughter rang far across the evening
air.

On another trip, Jack was finding it hard to
concentrate on Mrs. Gullion's good food. His
mind was on the sheaves of oats in the little field
he had passed on the way in. Gullion, knowing
his friend's devious ways, waited until dark,
then went out and lay in his field, determined to
put up with the discomfort in order to capture
and beat up The Ripper. He had worked very
hard that day, though, and soon fell asleep. The
red glow of the rising sun awakened him and, as
usual, several of his stooks were missing. It was
Jack's turn to laugh.

Half-Way House, the place my parents were now
approaching, was famous throughout the country. Stage coaches
stopped at the large, two-storeyed building, and behind the
house were several good cabins equipped with kitchens. Mr.
Eggie was reputed to be the wealthiest farmer in the district.
While being seated at a long table, Mother expressed her surprise
at its size, saying, "There must be sixteen or seventeen of us
around this table!" Mrs. Eggie laughed, "Before the railway,
there were often thirty gathered around it!"

Leaving Eggie's, my parents came down from the heights for
a short while, as the trail wound its way between the bridge
lakes (Bouchard and Jolicoer) before climbing the height of land
separating the Mackenzie and Saskatchewan watersheds. From
this point, all waters flow to the Arctic Ocean. As one old timer
so aptly put it, "After that you would think everything would be

39

down hill going," for right away the trail had to cross Stony Creek which, a short distance west, joins the Tawatinaw River and flows down 150 feet to the valley below.

But for the next twenty miles, the trail kept to the higher ground until it came to the present town of Meanook. Halfway between Meanook and Perryville, they passed another popular stopping place run by Mrs. Lewis, whose descendants, at last report, are still living there. Again they had to descend to the valley, to cross the west side of the Tawatinaw. It was the steepest hill they had encountered so far, and to Mother it looked more like a mountain. Several rigs were ahead of them, watching as two outfits slowly wound their way down. Before a sleigh could descend, its runners needed chainlocking, to prevent the loads from crashing into the heels of the teams.

Here, Mother and Dad caught up with Sam, who was next in line to go down. He introduced two of his friends; they would help my father with his attempt. Then Sam disappeared over the top of the hill. Noticing Mother's tense, white face, Sam's friends told her that this little "molehill" was nothing to worry about and soon had her laughing with them. Before she knew it, they were safely down.

Mother watched the sunset fade, leaving the sky an inky black. The jewel-like stars hung so low that she imagined she could pluck them one by one. It was just before crossing the Tawatinaw that they caught sight of the lights they had been watching for. Mother, peering into the night, could barely make them out. At first they appeared as a small village with still another huge hill overshadowing it. It was known as Smith's Hill, Dad said, and it was a reminder that this would be their last night on the Athabasca Trail.

The regular freighters, Dad told her, looked forward to spending the night at Billy Smith's place, for they could always rely on shelter for themselves and their teams. Billy, who had been a freighter once himself, had seen to that, for he had experienced the hardship of long cold days on the trail, never knowing if he would find accommodation at the day's end. Dad was told that Smith had driven himself relentlessly, making a record fourteen trips in 1905 from Athabasca Landing to Edmonton. His establishment could now put up sixty teams and also offered clean, first-class cabins. "Besides," Dad said, "Billy's wife always has a good hot meal ready for travellers."

After their meal, the guests always sat around the fire in the Smith's big parlour, enjoying each other's company. Billy, himself a great storyteller, entertained his guests for hours, telling of adventures from the great fund of knowledge he had acquired over the years. It was not surprising that freighters often left feed for their teams and continued the nine miles to Athabasca Landing, then after unloading, would go back and spend the night with the Smiths. Dad said that he had often done the same.

On his last trip, Dad mentioned to Billy that the next time he came through he would be on his way to Grouard with his wife and eighteen-month-old son. Billy remembered from previous talks with Dad that it would be quite an experience for Mother, who had always lived in a city, and told his wife Bessie. She spoke to Dad the next morning, inviting him and his family to spend the night with them when they came through.

Dad's team must have been recognized, for as they pulled in Billy came striding out to meet them. Mother smiled when she saw several children trailing behind him, as well as two dogs and a cat, while his wife admonished her noisy brood from the doorway. The boys soon had the sleigh unloaded and the team attended to. While the girls took charge of Carlton, Billy gallantly helped Mother into the house. Here she was given a warm welcome by Bessie Smith, an attractive red-haired woman, only six years older than she. Mother found it difficult to believe that Bessie was the mother of these half-grown children. Billy, noticing her incredulous expression, laughed, saying that he was used to having his wife taken for his daughter. He then strode out to greet a freighter who was just pulling in.

Soon they were seated and enjoying an excellent meal. Billy had eaten earlier with the hired men and freighters, as was his custom. Mother complimented her hostess, saying that she thought she did not like moosemeat, but this roast was delicious.

With a smile in her voice, Bessie explained that there was a trick to cooking wild game. "It needs to be basted often," she said, "and strips of salt pork or bacon wrapped around it works wonders, as it is drier than domestic meat." Mother was to remember this, but it was the recipe for Bessie's rhubarb and saskatoon pudding that she happily tucked away.

"I'm glad that you arrived later," Bessie told my parents. "The girls and I had time to clear up after serving twenty people."

Dad asked how they managed, thinking of the work as well as getting the provisions for feeding a crowd like this every day.

"We have a large garden and chickens, pigs, turkeys, and domestic rabbits. It is a lot of work," Bessie admitted. "But the children help, Billy sees to that, and with a hired girl now and then, we manage. Philip, our oldest son, has been working like a man, clearing brush by hand since he was nine." With a look of pride, she indicated a sturdy lad of fifteen. However, the children were deprived of formal education at that time, for the Meanook school was not built until a few years after my parents' visit, and by that time Philip had left home. He went to work in Edmonton, where he managed eventually to get some schooling.

After supper Mother and Dad sat in front of the fireplace, as many guests had before, listening to Billy Smith's stories. The Smiths were the first white settlers in the district. Mother was pleased to meet the outstanding pioneer and wanted to hear his experiences first hand. She was also anxious to learn more about Bessie. She felt a strong kinship towards this soft-spoken woman with red hair that shone like burnished gold in the firelight. Billy was happy to oblige.

Originally from Sarnia, Ontario, Billy had been sent up the Athabasca River to drill an oil well as part of an Imperial Oil team. He was only seventeen at the time and anxious to learn all about this northern river, on whose banks Athabasca Landing was built. He became familiar with every foot of it while tracking the scows from Fort Resolution – 725 miles in 28 days. One of his many adventures was building the world's smallest railway on an island in order to move freight around the Pelican

Rapids. He was later given the job as engineer on the Northern Transport's *Grahame*, at the time John Gullion was captain of the boat. They became friends, and the captain brought Billy home for one of his wife's good meals. This is how he became acquainted with Bessie, the captain's daughter. Although she was only fifteen at the time and he was thirty-one, they fell in love and were married.

Elizabeth Gullion was only seven when she and her family trekked a thousand miles across the prairies and bushlands from Fort Gary to the Lower Settlement, later known as Strathcona, in a long caravan of Red River carts. These carts were to our Canadian prairies what the covered wagon was to the western United States. Constructed entirely of wood with a deep box slung between two great wheels, the Red River cart could carry up to eight hundred pounds and was drawn by an Indian pony or oxen. Its worst feature was the continuous squeal of the axle. The piercing noise shattered the air and made conversation impossible.

When asked about the journey, Bessie had this to say:

"Except when it rained, we children had a wonderful time. Whenever we grew tired of bumping along in the cart, we climbed over the tailgate and ran behind. I still remember the velvety feel of warm dust squishing between my toes.

"The time we looked forward to the most was Saturday night, for as a rule we did not travel on Sunday and could sleep until later. The scouts, having been over the trail previously, led us to a good campsite near a lake or stream, protected by a wooded area. If luck was with us, we pulled in early on this special night. Our mothers had plenty to do before we started out again on Monday. While most of the men were setting up camp, a few axemen, along with the children looked for deadfall. Old stumps and trees shattered by lightning a few summers ago, soon became blazing fires.

"After the meal was over and the infants tucked away, the children were allowed to stay up for a while. Then as the fires burned low and the stars came out, the fiddlers began to play and feet began to tap. Sometimes there was dancing, but everyone always ended up singing the old songs and hymns, handed down from one generation to another."

Bessie said she could never remember falling asleep on these nights, but in the morning she was curled up in the little nest her mother had prepared for her.

"My wife was only sixteen when Philip was born," Billy told them. "And although her mother was with her, she was also attended by Mrs. Plant, a native herb doctor and midwife. It was not long before Bessie became her assistant, learning her skills. When Mrs. Plant could no longer travel over the rough trails, Bessie carried on, and for many years delivered most of the babies in the district. Ethel Brown, who resides with her husband on a farm in the Meanook district, was delivered by Bessie Smith, as was her sister Gwen. After both deliveries, Bessie stayed on and helped their mother for a week. However, she was unable to do this when their brother, Arthur, was born, since her own son, Frank, was born exactly a week later.

Mrs. Brown was only thirteen when this good neighbour died of diabetes. But, as she said a while ago, "I'll always remember those happy times we shared with the Smiths, and the wonderful food for which Bessie was famous."

Billy was a father figure for the entire district. During the 1918 flu epidemic he and another local man, Harry Stoper, saved many lives, providing food, wood, and water for the sick and helping Bessie to nurse them when necessary. After donating land for a cemetery, he and his hired men planed lumber for caskets, which he donated to those who could not afford to buy them.

Billy was also a good carpenter and has been given credit for the construction of the building that still houses the *Athabasca Echo*. A year after his marriage, he and Bessie decided to take up farming and built their home and stopping house at the foot of the big hill that would be known as Smith's Hill. Out of necessity, a blacksmith shop was added to his establishment. He owned the first thrashing machine thereabouts, with a huge engine that was said to have been "as long as a barn." His own large fields took several weeks to thrash and, he said, getting the machine up the steep hill to thrash his neighbours' crops often took him days in wet weather.

"His next venture was a sawmill and planer. Most of the lumber used by the homesteaders around here was planed by Billie," Bessie volunteered.

"It's common knowledge," Dad said, turning to Mother, "that most of the settlers stopping here had intended going farther afield. They never got any farther. Billy and Bessie talked them into becoming their neighbours and have been taking care of them ever since." They all laughed.

"Bessie," said her husband, "stuck to her principles a while back, refusing to serve two young RCMP officers on their way to Edmonton with a prisoner until they untied the man and brought him in, saying that no one ever left her door without being fed."

A bit embarrassed at finding herself the centre of attention, Bessie was glad when the subject changed to the most important topic of the day in the north – the railway that had reached Athabasca Landing the previous summer. Billy said it had brought a substantial growth to the town. Homesteaders, businessmen, professionals, and tradesmen were pouring into the north. Dad was excited at the prospect of the railway reaching Grouard. He admitted he had bought a hotel there, sight unseen. Mother, the more practical of the two and a better judge of character than Dad, had her suspicions about the hotel. It would be a while before he would come to value his wife's judgement.

CHAPTER SIX

Music in the Night

I t was late, almost eight A.M., when my parents woke up the next morning, stretching in their soft, clean bed. The tantalizing smell of freshly-brewed coffee drifted up to them. Knowing their visitors had only nine miles to travel to Athabasca Landing that day, the Smiths had let them sleep in.

After a breakfast of ham, eggs, homemade bread, and chokecherry jelly, Mother and Dad reluctantly bid goodbye to their hosts, promising to return for a visit – in a year or two. It would be almost a decade before Mother would pass that way again, en route for Calgary. It would be even longer, close to twenty-five years, before Dad visited the outside world. That was to watch my brother, Wilbur Junior, ride in the Calgary Stampede at the age of nineteen, after winning the Peace River-Grande Prairie Championship Belt. Only Dad's fatherly pride could induce him to leave the farm during that busy period of his life.

It was just as well my parents had not hurried that morning, for several rigs waited ahead of them to climb the long hill. It was a slow process as each of the rigs had to be double-teamed, with one man walking beside the sled, ready to shove the steel dog – a device with sharp prongs that dug into the snow to slow the sleigh down on steep inclines – under the runners if the load started to pull the team and sled back downhill. Everyone was caught up in the excitement while the horses struggled slowly upward. Sweat trickled down their flanks as they strained every muscle. The drivers shouted encouragement to the teams, putting their shoulders to the load when necessary. Although the trail wound upwards in hairpin turns, the incline was still very steep, and the men rested their teams at least a dozen times as they rounded the sharp curves on the mile-long trek to the top. There was a general air of animation and the men were cheerful, joking and laughing, as they helped each other and shouted out encouragement to the other drivers. A lusty cheer was heard as each hard-pressed team finally made it safely to the top.

While Dad and Sam helped the less experienced drivers, Mother joined the two women waiting in the sled ahead. They were Mary Reid, like mother expecting a child in late summer, and her sister-in-law Sally, a plump, vivacious woman in her mid-thirties. Mary and her husband were headed for the High Prairie region where they planned to homestead; Sally, a teacher, had been promised a one-room school nearby. They were following Sally's other brother who had come out two years earlier with his wife and had written that after working hard to clear their land, they had planted a small field which, with its yield of green feed along with the wild hay they had harvested, had provided enough fodder for their horses and a cow. They were also proud of the bountiful crop of vegetables they had planted and mentioned the wild berries and wild flowers that grew in profusion. Their neighbours had pitched in to help them build a sturdy cabin, large enough to accommodate them all. Although the barn was small in order to conserve heat, it could be added to, and they were now anxiously awaiting the arrival of their relatives.

Both women were from rural Ontario farm families and, although they realized hard work lay ahead of them, were looking forward to their new lives with great anticipation. Sally explained to Mother that she only decided to join her brother and sister-in-law on the long trek west at the last minute. Mary laughed teasingly, then added, "I think it was the good-looking bachelor friend my brother-in-law wrote about, rather than a true pioneer spirit that made Sally decide to come with us. In fact, he said single women are very rare in this neck of the woods and she could expect to have more than one suitor."

Sally blushed through her tan as her good-natured laugh rang out. She had had the responsibility of caring for her mother, an invalid who had died just a year ago, she said, and this had kept her from marrying.

"But, if the right man pops the question, I'd be more than ready to say yes."

The women's sleigh began its slow ride uphill and Mother waved a reluctant goodbye to her new friends. These women had come from a vastly different background from hers. Yet, for a brief moment, their lives had touched as they travelled the same path. They had promised to write to each other, but Mother realized their lives would be full and busy over the next few years and it would be a long time, if ever, before they met again.

Some forty years later, an elderly couple came to my parents' market garden to buy vegetables. The woman looked vaguely familiar. It was Sally, plumper and white-haired, but still vivacious and now the proud grandmother of five. Mary's story had not ended as happily. Her husband had answered the call to arms during the First World War and died in France. For a few years she had tried to run their small farm herself, before returning to Ontario with her young daughter. She never remarried.

They could see that an outfit on the hill was in trouble, with one of the horses down. The sleigh was saved from sliding back over the embankment by the quick action of the driver's partner, who shoved the steel dog under the runners. He then threw his weight behind the heavy load while two men rushed to help. The horse had thrown a shoe and was led stumbling downhill to be reshod while another team was brought up to pull the rig to the side of the narrow trail.

Reid's sleigh made it safely to the top. Sam's outfit, however, needed assistance several times before it disappeared over the crest of the hill.

The sun shone on the dappled coats of Dad's team; with tossing heads they started up the hill, drawing a murmur of approval from the watching horsemen. It was not every day they had a chance to see a pair of matched Clydesdales such as these. Dad had paid two thousand dollars for them (a great deal of money in those days) but, as he often said, "they were worth every dollar of it." Their great strength, as well as the rhythm in their stride, was standing them in good stead, for although the steep hill was very icy after so many teams had trod its surface, they were making good progress. Then Babe faltered, slipped, and was down on one knee. Dad jumped to his feet, yelling encouragement. With a mighty pull of the reins, Babe was up. The sleigh had only slipped back a foot or so, but they were on the outmost bend and the slope fell sickeningly before them to the valley floor. Dad was out in a flash, throwing Mother the reins. She was able to keep the horses' heads up while he inserted the steel dog, taking some of the strain off Girlie. He soon found a ball of ice wedged in Babe's hoof, protruding far enough to prevent the shoe from getting a grip and quickly removed it. He gave a sigh of relief when they rounded the last crest.

At the top, they pulled the rig to the side of the trail behind Sam's to rest the horses and gazed out over the level plateau, broken only by light stands of willow and low bushes. It was a welcome sight after the hilly, heavily-wooded countryside they were leaving behind. Brownie was let out to run while they ate their lunch and, disappearing into the bush, she let out a series of excited barks. Grabbing their rifles, Sam and Dad followed her. The sound of shots cracked out on the frosty air and the men reappeared, very pleased with themselves as they held up two partridges. Brownie trotted behind wearing a silly grin.

Meanwhile, Carlton's face was getting very red, and Mother noticed her fingers and nose were beginning to tingle. The sun was shining brightly but she was amazed when Dad told her it was 20° F below zero. Even after living two years in Alberta, she could still be fooled by the northern weather – the cold did not seem to penetrate, even at minus 35° F, when the sun was shining.

The hill above Athabasca Landing offered a magnificent view of the town, nestled in the valley in the protecting arms of the high hills. At its feet the wide river wound northward as far as the eye could see. Mother was excited by the prospect of being in a real town again. But first, they had to get down one last hill, so steep a pioneer woman had written the town was aptly named Athabasca Landing, as just getting to the bottom could be called a "landing." As the men helped each other fasten heavy chains around the sleigh runners in order to gouge the icy hill, Mother looked at the town below. They had learned a little about its background from the Smiths.

For years the population of Athabasca Landing had been no more than a few hundred. The early settlers took pride in their town; they had built sturdy dovetailed buildings and painted the roofs bright green or red. Quite recently this had changed, with the population nearly doubling. The Hudson's Bay Company had been granted certain sections of land in each new settlement and was now charging exorbitant prices for this land. Thus the dwellings were only temporary tar-paper shacks or tents, until such time as the company could force their inhabitants to pay for the land on which at first only small deposits were made. Still, Mother thought it a pretty sight, nestled in the hills beside the river. After travelling through a hundred miles of wilderness, it seemed quite a place. The spirals of smoke curled upwards into the darkening sky, and just as they reached town, lights began to twinkle, like welcoming beacons.

They were pleased with their accommodation. The couple who owned the stopping house lived upstairs, and the wife offered to care for Carlton the next day, giving Mother a chance to explore the town. "Don't hurry back," this good-natured woman told them, "I'll feed him along with my children." Dad explained to Mother as they left that he and Sam had often stayed there because the hotel, since prohibition had been lifted, had become a place for drunken brawls.

Their first stops were at the big trading posts – the Hudson's Bay and Revillon Frères – where Dad put in a supply order and Mother purchased warmer clothing. She was fascinated by the variety of goods – large open bins of flour, salt, beans, and oatmeal, every imaginable kind of cooking utensil, huge slabs of bacon suspended from the ceiling, ready-made clothing, and yard goods.

At one end of the store, the post buyer was examining a catch of fur, just brought in by some Indians. When Mother admired a soft, dark silvery pelt, Dad told her it was silver fox. At the yard goods section, a group of shy, Native women with smooth skins and jet-black braids selected fabrics from the bright-hued cottons and ginghams, while their button-eyed papooses watched the proceedings solemnly from their mothers' backs.

Outside in the street, a colourful assortment of humanity paraded by. The freighters, usually burly, self-confident men were recognizable by their long raccoon-skin coats. There were also a few farmers in from the homestead to buy supplies, Indians dressed in their winter moosehide, pioneers newly arrived off the trail and happy to be in a town again, and the townspeople hurrying about their business.

My parents looked over the boats hauled up on the shores of the river. Two of them were Mounted Police craft. My parents, noting their slim lines, decided they were built for speed as well as ruggedness – qualities necessary in the pursuit of bootleggers who smuggled kegs of beer and whiskey to Indians living in remote areas along the river.

Mother caught sight of her first dog team, magnificent animals with bushy tails curving over their backs like graceful plumes. The lead dog had a long, soft coat of grey, highlighted with touches of amber. The team's harness was trimmed with brightly-coloured pompoms, and bells jingled as they trotted along. Mother, afraid that they might disappear, pulled at Dad's coat sleeve until he realized what she wanted. He motioned to the tall young Métis driver to pull over. His name was Joseph Nadeau, and he agreed to give them a ride. The young man raised the dogs from birth, he proudly told my parents, as he tucked fur robes around them. Mother said she heard that Husky dogs were vicious and could not be trusted. His answer was that dogs are like people; if they are raised properly, they are loyal and gentle, and that even wolves had hardly ever been known to harm people. He added that some Indians and white men starved and beat their dogs, and this brought out the worst in the animals.

The dogs leapt forward with a burst of speed and swept around a curve, sending the snow flying. My parents laughed; they had not enjoyed themselves as much in a long time. After the ride, Dad asked Joseph to have lunch with them. His smile showed his pleasure, and they were soon seated in a small cafe.

Joseph was of mixed French, Scottish, and Cree heritage, a good-looking young man, tall and slim with the lithe movements of a sprinter. He had dark hair and eyes, and his complexion, also dark, had a ruddiness that spoke of exposure to wind and sun. His soft voice held a faint French accent. Mother noticed he was well-spoken and seemed to have had some education. He told them that his mother and father had both lost their parents in the 1870 smallpox epidemic, and had been raised and educated by the Grey Nuns at Father Lacombe's mission school. Here, along with their regular schooling, his father was taught the blacksmith trade, while his mother learned to cook and sew. Joseph's parents made sure that he and his sisters also received some schooling at the mission. He told Mother and Dad that he trapped in the winter and worked in his father's blacksmith shop during the summer. His father wanted him to go back to the mission school to learn a trade, but Joseph loved the life of the bush.

He described the little log cabin he built with the help of his father, twenty miles upriver. His dark eyes were expressive as he tried to make them understand how he felt as he left his cabin to tend his trapline on cold, crisp mornings, his snowshoes leaving wide tracks on the newly fallen snow, the silvery sickle of a moon fading in the hazy sky as the sun climbed higher above the spruce trees. There were moments, he said, when he felt the beauty of the land was created just for him, and he lifted his voice in a shout of joy. Some day, he said, he would stop trapping and return to the mission to learn a trade. But for now he was content. My parents nodded their agreement. Dad assured Joseph he understood, and that he too had experienced the same sense of awe when riding alone through the great, rolling South African veldt. The talk then turned to Dad's travels and adventures in Africa. Joseph's attention was absorbed as he listened in fascination.

Before bidding Joseph goodbye, Dad told him to weigh carefully his father's advice. With so many people pouring into the north, carpentry would be a good trade. He and Mother got up to leave, then Dad paused and turned back, saying he still had a business transaction to settle. But Joseph laughed and left without accepting payment for the ride.

Later in town, my parents met an older couple who were headed for Edmonton for a load of supplies. When the woman learned it was Mother's first trip to Grouard, she had some good advice for her. She told her to cook pots of stew or whatever they fancied and freeze them. It was much easier and faster to cut off a chunk and heat it up than to cook on the trail. There were few road houses along the miles ahead.

The next day in the early afternoon, Mother, having just finished cooking her pots of stew, had decided to have a rest when Dad arrived with three large whitefish he had bought for twenty-five cents each from a man in from Lesser Slave Lake. Before she could sarcastically ask who was going to cut them up and scale them, there was a knock on the door. Joseph and his sister Sarah and her little son walked in. They had come to say goodbye, knowing my parents were leaving in the morning. Mother asked if they would like the fish, as she could not possibly prepare them for use on the trail before leaving. Sarah said a few words in French to Joseph, and he put the fish into a sack, saying that he and his mother would have them all ready for cooking in the morning. He said his mother would be glad to do this; his parents were grateful to Dad for persuading him to return to the mission and study carpentry.

This was good news to my parents for they liked the young Métis. Dad, knowing it was a difficult choice, said, "I don't blame you for wanting to hang on to the life you love. But remember, wherever you live change is inevitable. Some of the saddest men I've known have been those unable to change."

Sarah took a small package from her pocket and shyly handed it to Mother, saying, "I just finished these for my little boy, but I'd like you to have them for your son." Opening the package, mother found a small pair of moccasins that fit Carlton perfectly. They were made of tanned moosehide, with little flaps that came up to the calves and wrapped and tied with a rawhide cord. They were beautifully trimmed with beadwork on blue velvet. Mother had been unable to find moccasins to fit him and was delighted. They were warmer and softer than his heavy boots and she remembered, too, how he kicked her with them every time he climbed up and down the seat of the sleigh.

Carlton loved the new moccasins and sat on the bed delightedly pulling them on and off while Sarah's son watched solemnly until Dad laced them up. While the grownups enjoyed the tea and cake Mother served, the two children raced up and down the room.

The next morning was cold and clear as Babe and Girlie picked their way down the high earth bank to the river below. The rolling whiteness of the Athabasca was relieved by the dark trail, twisting and curving with the shoreline. The sun would not be up for a while, but in the soft glow of the fading moon, the scenery held a fragile beauty. They passed a little island densely covered with spruce, then, turning left, followed along the shore where roots of snow-laden trees clung precariously to the bank above. After the treacherous hills, Dad thought the river trail would be a cinch, although the heavy snowfall of the past few days could slow them down.

Sam and Brownie were no longer with them. He had left for Grouard when he heard of a chance to pick up a good team from a homesteader who was leaving. He said that he regretted deserting them, but if he were to continue freighting he would need a better team. Promising to take good care of Brownie, he had gone ahead. Mother and Dad travelled for an hour or two with the blue jays for company. Ahead, two outfits were travelling close together. A man handled the first rig while his wife drove the second one. Pulling over, the young man asked Dad for a cigarette, though he probably only wanted to break the monotony of the trail with a chat while resting the teams.

My parents looked with admiration at the young woman driving her team with apparent ease. When Mother commented on her courage, she admitted that she had not planned it, but an extra rig was needed to bring their farm equipment and winter supplies. Looking mischievously at her husband, she said, "A lot of men's jobs aren't any more difficult than women's."

Her husband was quick to reply, "I have to admit that my wife is an improvement over the driver of a rig we saw travelling with a group crossing Lesser Slave Lake. They had propped a scarecrow made from an old suit of clothes stuffed with straw and tied it to the seat of the sleigh so the horses would think they had a driver." He laughed, adding, "It seemed to be working."

After they left, Mother could not help wondering how the young wife would manage the icy hills ahead, not realizing that the steep river banks she had already encountered had been nearly as frightening. Pioneer women, Mother would learn, performed many tasks they would have thought themselves incapable of, and she would be no exception.

The team was making good time, much to Dad's relief. It was a long haul to the stopping house operated by an Indian family, and he no longer travelled a familiar route. The prospect of spending the night with his family on the wind-swept river chilled him more than the cold north wind.

It was past noon, and the sun was beginning to warm the snow-bound earth, when they noticed a small island in the distance near the trail. They decided to lunch in its shelter. It was farther than it appeared, but they were glad they had waited. With a huge spruce tree sheltering them, they were able to remove their mittens to eat Mother's fried chicken. The March sun melted the snow causing it to drip from the branches and send out a spicy aroma. The aroma brought back memories to Mother of past Christmases and the small, thin trees she had thought so wonderful. Gazing at this giant, its branches reaching towards the sky, she found it hard to believe that they were of the same species. She contemplated her husband – this man who had trekked all over the world, far from big cities – and it occurred to her that he was not just seeking adventure but, like the tree, he needed space and sunshine in order to put down roots and grow.

After finishing lunch, Dad persuaded Mother to crawl into the back of the rig with Carlton for a nap, as she might have to relieve him later. The truth of the matter was, he was worried and needed time to sort out his thoughts. Slapping the reins on the team's rumps, he went over the conversation he had with the couple they had just met. He remembered that when he asked about the Grouard hotel or its former owner, the young man seemed evasive, saying they had only passed the hotel a few times and had never been acquainted with the Myers. His reluctance gave Dad an uneasy feeling. Added to this, as they were starting off the young man called after him, "If this hotel doesn't pan out, there's plenty of good land near us, and we'd love to have you for neighbours." Dad had not noticed Mother's reaction, but knowing little escaped her, he felt that she was worried too. Before leaving Edmonton she had been doubtful about their buying a hotel sight unseen.

Mother awoke to the rhythmical sound of horses' hooves on the hardpacked snow. The cold wind hit her as soon as she sat up. Quickly pulling a woolen hat over her forehead and knotting a big scarf behind her coat collar, she was able to shield her face. Looking out, she noted from the long blue shadows descending the hills that it would soon be dark. She gazed down at her sleeping child, wondering how she could have let herself be persuaded to bring him through this vast wilderness. Determined to banish her doubts, she crawled up beside Dad.

"We should reach the stopping house within the next two hours," he told her as he handed her the reins. He tried to warm himself, whacking his hands together and stamping his feet to bring back the circulation. He had just dozed off, when the cry of a wolf rent the air, filling the river valley with its haunting sound. It rose loud and sharp, then as abruptly as it had begun, broke off. Father grabbed the reins as the team leapt forward, no longer needing to be prodded. Dad was just assuring Mother that a single wolf would never attack, when the answering cry of its mate sounded from far off in the hills. All was quiet for a few seconds, then a chorus of howls filled the air. More voices joined in until the entire pack seemed to be harmonizing in a wild chorus of untamed music.

Dad pulled up the team and they sat listening to the wolves, while shivers sent tingles up their spines. The great sky was filled with glittering stars so close they could almost touch them. The moon climbed above the hills, causing the snow around them to sparkle like the sky above. The chorus ended abruptly and Dad urged the team on. They no longer felt the cold. Huddled close under the robes, they rode in silence as the miles slipped by. When they reached a fork in the trail, they could just make out dim lights on a hill above the river. Mother forgot that she had dreaded sleeping in an Indian stopping house. Her only worry now was that there might not be room for them.

Dad's concern was for his big horses. An oldtimer told him that staying at a Native bunkhouse had nearly cost him his team: the temperature had plunged to 60° below zero that night and he discovered that the barn – built for the small Indian ponies – was too low for his horses to enter. To keep their feet from freezing, he had wrapped them in gunny sacks and spent most of the night walking them.

Mother was alarmed when she caught sight of the trail that sloped sharply upward towards the steep riverbank. Dan told her to bring Carlton up with them, warning her that if the sleigh started to slip back she would have to jump out and put the steel dog under the runners. Although steep, it was but a short distance up the bank, and their tired team made it safely to the top. The fierce din of barking dogs grew louder as they approached the stopping house. Mother was glad to see that the animals were tethered by chains to small dog houses.

The main building was long and low with bunkhouses on one side. Several freighters' sleighs were pulled up in front of the bunkhouses, which looked as if they were all occupied. The door of the main building flew open and a dark youth raced out, pulling on his moosehide jacket as he ran towards the dogs. Yelling loudly in Cree, he hurled a large stick into their midst. He said his name was Louis, and told them his mother sent him to say the bunkhouses were full but they were welcome to spread their bed rolls on the floor of the family cabin. Carlton, taking him for Joseph Nadeau, held out his arms. Louis picked him up and headed for the cabin, leaving Dad to help Mother. She was stiff and cold from sitting for hours and could hardly walk.

While Dad attended to the team, Mother and Carlton sat on the bed roll and watched Louis stoke the big drum heater. He shoved a long log into the roaring fire and caused a billowing of smoke and sparks that delighted the small boy.

Peering through the smoky haze, Mother saw that the house consisted of one large room, with a kitchen at the back and bedrooms curtained off on either side. The cabin's peeled logs seemed well chinked, but the wind was coming through the door made of split poles tapered to fit as snugly as possible, although a large moose hide hung over it. Mother watched gusts of wind billow it back and forth. Split poles pounded into the earth made a fairly smooth floor. Two small windows provided light by day; just now a kerosene lamp in a wall bracket revealed a sparsely furnished room containing a table with benches around it, a cookstove, a washstand made of orange crates, and a few shelves. Several sets of moose and deer antlers held rifles, snowshoes, and heavy outer garments.

When Mother started to move her bed roll back from the heat of the stove, Louis stopped her, saying, "Don't move, the green logs have plenty sap. They won't get hot now, but later when it's very cold, they'll burn like hell. Plenty warm here then." She smiled her thanks, feeling the heat relax her tired body, while the tantalizing smell of venison stew filled the room and roused her appetite.

Shouts from men wheeling their dog teams into the yard set the dogs barking again. With a flurry of snow, the door opened ushering in a group of Indians returning from selling their furs at the Athabasca Landing post. They trooped in, stashing their gear not far from where Mother and Carlton sat. She forgot her hunger as she watched these strange men. Remembering the wild west movies she had seen at their Omaha theatre, with scenes of Indian raids where helpless settlers were scalped in their beds, sent a chill up her spine. The feeling became more intense when she saw that they carried rifles and that handles of long knives protruded from their belts. Then fear turned to amazement when she noticed an older man with a violin tucked under his arm.

Later, being seated at the long table gave my parents a good view of the Natives as they filed past. Most of them were dressed entirely in moosehide, from moccasins to pants and jackets, although two younger men wore jackets of creamy white elkhide, set off by exquisite floral beadwork that trimmed all their jackets and moccasins. Two of the men wore suit coats over their jackets and, from the interest shown by Louis and his mother and sister, Mother decided they were recent purchases. The men were especially proud of all the pockets. Their long hair was held back by strips of moosehide. Dad asked Mother if she was afraid. She smiled and whispered back that marrying a man from the wilds of Africa had prepared her for sleeping next to these Indians.

When the meal was over and Mother had finished feeding Carlton, she noticed that the Indian party was taking quite an interest in the boy. Louis confirmed her suspicions by asking if he could take him over to his friends for a closer look. As Louis carried him toward the Natives, his mother and sister followed. My parents watched as the Indians looked with awe at their beautiful child with his pink-and-white complexion, blue eyes, and curling golden hair.

Mother was a light sleeper and was disturbed later in the night by the sound of the door opening and thought she saw two men enter, but she fell back to sleep. She was roused again by the smell of rum drifting over as the men passed around a bottle. Seeing by the light of the fire that my parents were awake, the men lit the lamp and called the women and Louis. Sounds of an argument could be heard. Shortly after, Louis and the two women appeared carrying a drum. Everyone was soon in high spirits. The drum began to throb and the violin joined in, squealing out a lively tune – the *moochigan* had begun. The group beckoned to Mother and Dad to join them. My parents smiled and shook their heads but, since sleep was impossible, settled back to watch the fun.

The younger woman was the first to choose a partner, leading a youth to the middle of the floor where he began a lively jig around her, while she, looking very grave, jumped up and down, both feet together. Her mother followed and then the men paired off until all were dancing with great vigour. Mother was sure she would not sleep another wink that night but, lulled by the monotonous beat of the drum and the soft shuffle of moccasined feet, felt her eyes grow weary and soon drifted off again.

When she and Dad woke the next morning, they were amazed to discover their Native friends had fed the dogs and silently gone away. The coals in the kitchen stove were still live. They quickly ate and got ready for the road. Dad left a generous payment and, like the Indians, they slipped away leaving their hosts to sleep off the night of revelry.

CHAPTER SEVEN

Time for Union Suits

They were down the grade. Dad decided not to chainlock the sleigh's runners as the gravel on the hill, mixed with snow and ice, made a natural brake. In the distance they could see a large number of rigs. Mother would have liked to join them, but Dad pointed out that they were travelling at too fast a pace. He told her not to worry though, as Moose Portage, where they would spend the night, was the largest Indian village between Athabasca and Grouard and had quite a number of good stopover cabins. It was still a fair distance but they should make it before evening.

The sleigh's runners slid silently over the well-packed snow with only an occasional bump as they hit a ridge, and the whipple tree chains that connected the sleigh's round wooden bars to the horses' harness and collars tinkled a pleasant accompaniment to the rhythmic beat of their hooves. They were passing through great stands of spruce and jackpine, stretching as far as the eye could see in an unbroken mass of green. Dad had never seen forests like this before. He had been a youth when he left the farm, but he remembered that the kind of sandy soil on which these trees thrived did not produce good crops. Yet, he had been advised good farmland would start just before they reached Sawridge (now known as Slave Lake) and would continue through to the Peace River Country. He thought again of the couple they had met on the trail and the man's parting remark that there was good agricultural land to be had in the Grouard district if the hotel did not pan out.

Dad was beginning to wonder why his last business ventures had gone wrong, especially after he had done so well in South Africa. But in that country most of his business dealings had been with men whose reputations he had known. He found that by being honest and aboveboard, he had received the same treatment. This had not been the case in North America. He was starting to realize it was his impulsive nature that prompted him to invest in people and projects before they were thoroughly investigated. His wife had tried to point this out when they discussed buying another hotel, but he had not listened to her. Because Dad had spent his formative years in South Africa in a male-dominated society he had not heeded her advice. He smiled a bit ruefully as he glanced down at her, noticing that she too was deep in thought.

Mother liked these early mornings best, when the air was crisp and clear and everything seemed to sparkle. Carlton was settling into a routine, content to cuddle between his parents, the thick buffalo robe pulled up to his chin. Rounding a bend, Dad spotted a red fox digging for mice in the earth under the snow. The sleigh drew closer and the fox bounded up the steep bank, his golden red coat and white-tipped, bushy tail gleaming in the sun. At the top he turned and examined them with a look of curiosity on his pixie face. Carlton was wide awake and calling for Brownie, before remembering that the dog was no longer with them.

From his rough map, Dad thought they should be near a stopping place. Mother had made enough food to last several days and they carried extra feed for the horses in case of an emergency, but every teamster knew that horses should be stabled for an hour and a half at midday in rough weather, and they all needed the comfort and warmth these stopping places offered.

A few miles farther and the stopping place came into view, perched high on the bank. They were soon up the grade, the team attended to, and digging into a piping hot meal of roast moose meat and vegetables, topped off with stewed dried peaches and bannock.

The short northern day was drawing to a close and, as the twilight faded into darkness, a more intense cold crept in. Wrapping the reins around the post, Dad put an arm around Mother and settled deeper into the warm robe. They watched silently as the first star appeared, followed by another, then another, until the sky was filled with brightness. Babe and Girlie had become dark, shadowy forms blending into the night and only their familiar horsey sounds drifted back to them. The sleigh seemed to be floating. My parents were startled every now and then by the loud screech of the runners on the hard-packed snow, a sound that could be heard for a quarter of a mile on a cold night.

Mother sighed with relief when Dad pointed out pinpoints of light ahead. The long day on the trail would soon be at an end. The team did not need urging now; they anticipated the warm stable and good feed of oats, as well as the brisk rub-down Dad was never too tired to give them.

When they pulled into the stopping place at Moose Portage, a tall well-built Native came out of his cabin. He led them to one of the bunkhouses where a knock brought a middle-aged couple to the door. They were introduced as Robert and Joan Andrews. After explaining that all the cabins were filled, the Indian, Deome Gibeault, added that he could move his own family into a teepee if the Andrews did not want to share the accommodation. However, the couple insisted Mother and Dad stay with them that night, saying there was plenty of room and they were glad of the company. Taking it for granted that the issue was settled, they stepped out and helped carry in the grub box and other supplies. Then Mr. Andrews volunteered to help Dad stable his horses.

Mother expressed pleasure at finding a warm cabin with a good fire blazing in the mud fireplace. Mrs. Andrews said they had arrived only half an hour ago, but that the daughters of the family who operated the stopping place had kept the fires going most of the day. Mother examined the fireplace, called a mud fire chimney, with great care. It was circular and roughly four feet in diameter, built of plastered mud in the cabin's corner. Constructed of four upright poles held together with cross-pieces, hung with long mud-covered pieces of grass and coated with clay, it extended from the floor to some distance above the roof. A whole log had been placed upright in the chimney, and as the bottom burned off it dropped down, eliminating the need for frequent stoking. The hearth was made of flat stones.

Looking helplessly at the blazing fire, Mother wondered how she was going to heat her frozen food, especially with a hungry infant to pacify. With an understanding smile Mrs. Andrews, a mother of four, offered to heat some soup for Carlton. She had learned the trick of freezing soup right in the frying pan years ago, she said, when her husband first started freighting. Mother watched as she unwrapped the pan. Then, setting it on the hearth, Mrs. Andrews raked the coals forward and soon had the soup ready for the baby.

Joan, as this friendly woman insisted Mother call her, and Mother were soon planning to share their food. Joan offered to fry the fish Mother said she did not have the energy to tackle. The secret, Joan explained, was to cook everything before the trip, even to frying the potatoes which were now warming on the hearth. Mother placed four slices of frozen bread between the wires of her toaster and holding it over the flames soon had them golden brown. Joan told her she was learning fast.

Robert Andrews and Dad came in from feeding the horses. Andrews told his wife he had just seen one of the finest matched teams in the country. "The Freeland's Clydesdales are dead ringers for the pure bred Percheron stallion William McCue brought in a few months ago." Andrews explained that McCue had been trying to find a brood mare in order to obtain a foal from the Percheron. As they talked, the good smells and sounds of food cooking over the fire and the warmth of unexpected friendship enveloped the group in a clear and bright circle of light in the homely little shack. Overhead, the stars glittered far away in the cold blue winter night.

Dad was pleased that the fish Mother had nearly rejected

was providing their main course and complimented Joan on its brown crispness. Mother had watched its preparation carefully. She was determined to accomplish this new art of cooking. Joan consoled her, saying she thought Mother was very courageous to be travelling the trail with a small child while expecting another.

Like many other men in the north, Robert Andrews had hauled freight during the winter months of his first six years in the Peace River Country. "So you see," he said, smiling at Mother, "Joan has had a lot of experience cooking on the trail, and we eat like kings, compared to the poor devils who worked as trackers for the sturgeon-head boats."

Trackers had the difficult job of pulling boats upstream by means of ropes as they walked alongside on the shore. Rations usually consisted of bannock and tea, and bacon that was mostly fat. This was cooked until the fat was rendered. Then, after removing the charred bits, the trackers dipped the bannock into the grease and wash it down with tea. Now and then they were fortunate enough to shoot a moose or deer, or even a few rabbits. But bannock, grease, and tea was their usual daily fare. However, things picked up for them when the scows began to transport passengers.

My parents had first heard of this trade from Joseph and Sara Nadeau, whose father had started off as a tracker. The two had recounted that their grandfather, a Métis from St. Paul, Minnesota, was one of the trackers hired to pull the Hudson's Bay York boat of Chief Factor Rowand up river from Fort Edmonton. The factor had as his guest Father Lacombe who, at the age of twenty-five, was en route for Lac St. Anne to take charge of his first mission. During the trip, Father Lacombe tried to intercede with Chief Factor Rowand on behalf of a tracker who became ill, but the good priest was severely reprimanded for his trouble. On arriving at Fort St. Anne, this man and Joseph's grandfather decided to stay with the young father at his mission.

The water route between Athabasca Landing and Grouard was more popular than the trail because of treacherous bogs, muskeg, and hordes of mosquitoes and bulldog flies that infested the land during the summer. According to early records, many horses travelling the land trail in the summer months became so hopelessly imbedded in the mire they were left to die. Babies also were victims; many became ill and were buried along the route, to the heartbreak of their parents.

The Hudson's Bay Company built the first steamboat to ply the Athabasca River, followed by Bishop Grouard's *St. Joseph* and, in due time, many others. The sturgeon-heads, York boats, and scows still proved to be the most practical craft since it was never a sure thing that the steamers would be able to navigate the Lesser Slave River. This could be done only during early summer's high water and even then navigation was risky. The captain and crew of the steamer *Athabasca* had recently had some bad moments while steaming down this winding little river in high water. For some reason, the pilot lost control and in a matter of seconds the boat's nose swung into the bank and she was wedged crossways, the river being narrower than her 165-foot length. The boat formed a dam across the river and the crew were hard put to get her free.

More than one steamer had been caught in these sluggish waters in late fall and frozen in for the winter, which meant the crew had to walk back to Mirror Landing and return with extra men to help pull the boat onto the bank. The alternative was a sixteen-mile portage over a dusty trail between Mirror Landing and Sawridge.

Somers Somerset, who travelled by water from Athabasca Landing to Peace River, leaves this account, in the James MacGregor book, *Land of Twelve Foot Davis* (Edmonton: Institute of Applied Art, 1952):

> The Sturgeon-head boat in which we were to
> travel, is one of the features of a country where
> rivers are the only highways. A Sturgeon-head
> somewhat resembles a canal barge, but is
> broader of beam and draws less water, having a
> flattened bow, from which it derives its name. It
> is usually sixty feet wide and eighty feet long.

We embarked and shoved off into the middle of the stream, and then proceeded up the middle of the river in most picturesque fashion. The crew of ten stood upon the thwarts and punted with long poles; the steerman, upon a platform in the stern guided the boat with an oar or sweep, trailing behind, whilst a man in the bow balancing the pole in the manner of a tightrope walker, pointed out the shoals and shallows with either end as they appeared to the right or left. After a time the current ran stronger and we disembarked the men who proceeded to tow us. Towing, or tracking, as it is called in the North, brings up before the English mind pictures of well-kept paths and neat white gates fitted with easy springs, but the shores of Athabasca or Slave River can boast none of these advantages, the country being thickly bushed and very rough; and nowhere for a hundred consecutive yards is there good going.

In tracking, two lines are used, three or four men being harnessed to each rope. Behind these walks another whose duty it is to free the line when it becomes caught in the bushes. These unfortunates stumble along through the underbrush or bruise their moccasined feet against the sharp rocks by the waterside, often up to their waist in water, always leaning on the rope, and frequently almost losing their balance when it gets entangled in some twisted root. Hour after hour they go steadily forward, only halting for food – in this fashion we moved up the little river until the lake was reached. The wind was blowing a gale the following morning so we did not make a start until well on into the day, when it had moderated a little. But the waves still ran high and the rain fell in torrents. The men, however, rowed in splendid style and we made a late camp on the northern shore. The strength and endurance of these men ... both Indian and halfbreed, is quite remarkable. Each oar of a Sturgeon-head boat weighs a hundred pounds, being of a great length and thickness but narrowing towards the end. The rowers place a pad under one foot, the leg being held nearly straight before them, with the other leg beneath the seat, they rise to a standing position, and then throwing their weight on the sweep, to get a short kickoff from the pad; they sink back to the bench, thus completing the stroke. The last part of the journey was along a shallow channel through the large swamp that lies below the Fort ... the haunt of innumerable ducks and other wild fowl. Turning slightly to the north, we unloaded the boats on the open shore in front of Slave Lake Post [now Grouard].

Friends of the Andrews made this trip while bringing a new baby home and they said the captain and crew did everything possible to ensure their comfort and safety. Their most pleasant memories were the times they were able to use the sails while crossing Lesser Slave Lake. For it was then the crew sang the old French-Canadian voyageur songs handed down by their ancestors.

As my parents listened to these stories, they realized they had left civilization behind at Athabasca Landing. There had been no easy way for these pioneers, whether they entered the country in summer over the sloughs and grassy trails, or by water, or in winter across the ice and snow. They listened as the Andrews told how they had watched this new country slowly open up as more and more families moved in and stayed.

That night, a loud crack shattered the silence of the small

cabin. Mother found herself sitting bolt upright in bed, her heart pounding as she struggled out of a deep sleep. Reaching over to shake Dad's shoulder she noticed he was half awake. He yawned and muttered that the noise meant it was getting colder making the building contract, and was asleep again before she could get any further explanations. She noticed it was bitterly cold.

She heard someone struggling into clothes and in the dim light cast by the dying flames recognized Robert Andrews as he approached the fireplace. She watched as he raked the coals together then threw a handful of dry kindling on them and waited patiently until the blaze was strong enough to ignite the large log. She could see him plainly now as he turned to warm his back, and she thought how handsome he looked with the firelight softening his features. It was then she realized he had pulled his woolen shirt over his union suit but had not bothered with his trousers. Suppressing a giggle, she thought how shocked Aunt Em would be if she knew her Ollie was gazing at a man in his underwear. Robert returned to his bed, and all was quiet except for the crackling and hissing of the green poplar logs from the fireplace.

They were all asleep except Mother. Dad never had any problems sleeping. Mother often said he was off before his head touched the pillow. She tried to relax and was just drifting off when she felt the flutter of new life cradled so close to her heart. Her thoughts went back to the night nearly two years ago when she had first had this experience. Then, she had awakened my father so they could share the miracle of the life sign of their first child. But they had been newly wed then, with very few responsibilities compared to their present situation. So, for the time being, she was content to know that all was progressing normally. Saying a silent prayer for their safety as they journeyed through this wild, new land, she turned gently in her cramped space and fell asleep.

Dad knew as soon as he opened his eyes the next morning that it was too late for the early start they had planned for that day. Pulling on his trousers, he made his way to the fireplace where Robert Andrews was placing the coffee pot over the live coals. Robert said that when he discovered the drop in temperature he had decided against an early start to avoid lung damage to the horses, reminding Dad it was only a short day's run to Mirror Landing.

My parents were glad now that they had taken the freighter's advice and bought warmer clothing. They probably would need them for the rest of the trip. Dad's extra union suit had been indispensable from the start and was the first article Mother reached for in the morning, pulling it on under her voluminous nightgown. Although it was a bit long for her short legs, she tucked the cuffs into her heavy socks and wrapped her moccasin flaps neatly over them to help keep her body heat from escaping.

While the men harnessed the teams, Joan said to Mother, "On mornings like this, I usually wear a pair of Robert's trousers under my skirt." So Mother dug out the pair she had bought at the Landing. But when she tried them on, she discovered they did not fit over the small bulge of her waistline. She yanked them down, only to have them slip past her knees. When they recovered from laughing, Mother asked, "Now what do I do?" "Make them fit with a piece of string," Joan answered. And, in two shakes of a lamb's tail, as Mother used to say, she threaded one end through the buttonhole and tied the other, around the button. Then in a more serious vein, Joan said, "Many farmers buy moosehide pants from the Indians. They're windproof and wear forever."

My parents were to learn another useful trick that morning. While packing their grub boxes, Mother noticed several boulders among the hot coals. "We use them for foot-warmers," Joan said. When wrapped in gunny sacks or old blankets, they hold the heat for hours. We also use them to support the small grill for the stove we carry for emergencies."

Robert, who had just returned from the barn with Dad, insisted they take their makeshift stove, saying, "Joan and I won't need it, we won't be crossing the lake." Dad agreed, and also took his advice and stashed a small pile of firewood under the seat. "You should always be prepared for the worst when crossing that lake," Robert said.

Joan, seeing Mother's worried face, said, "It's only a precaution. You will probably use the wood for your cookstove in Grouard, but it's best not to take chances." My parents found it hard to say goodbye to these good, helpful people.

Dad caught a glimpse of the trousers while helping Mother into the sleigh, and smiled his approval. They were both learning to take advice.

The winter sun climbed higher, casting a soft blue light on the flat snowy surface of the river. It's brightness was deceptive though, and they coughed as the sharp air hit their lungs. "This is the coldest day we've had so far," he told Mother. When she looked up, she was startled to see her Dad's eyebrows white with frost. And when he turned towards her, she exclaimed, "Wilbur, the tip of your nose is frozen!" "Well," he said, "it's not the first time. You'd both better stay under rug." Carlton was asleep. After laying him down in the back and covering him, she tied a woolen scarf around her face and handled the reins while Dad gently massaged his nose with his fur mitt until the whiteness disappeared.

Rounding the bend in the river, they saw in the distance many vehicles on the ice, giving the impression of a small village on the move. As they drew near they could make out a number of cabooses – box-like shelters built over large freight sleighs. These were grouped together. Just beyond, a shelter rigged of canvas and poles had been erected to protect the horses.

As Mother and Dad pulled in, they could see that the ice trail leading up the bank to Mirror Landing (present-day Smith) was covered with water. They looked at one another and their hearts sank as the implication hit home. Then they noticed that the men in the vehicles ahead were huddled together under their robes in their unhitched sleighs, while smoke drifted upward from the caboose stovepipes. They decided that the women must be inside with the children, preparing lunch. As they approached, two men came forward and told them an accident had happened earlier that day – a freighter almost lost his outfit. The turbulent little Slave River, dropping down to join the larger Athabasca River here, had caused the overflow ahead. This is the story they told my parents:

Two young freighters had pulled ahead of the cavalcade, anxious to reach Mirror Landing, the first village after a hundred miles of slow travelling. They were both single and looking forward to a bit of fun. Just a hot bath and a good meal would be great, but they also anticipated meeting friends and shooting some pool; a party or dance might merit them breaking out the bottle they had stashed away for just such an occasion.

They realized they should not be crossing under these conditions before the older freighters arrived, but decided to take a chance. Tim, the more adventurous of the two, proposed walking across first to test the ice. He was soon back saying, "It seems solid enough and the water isn't deep." As he climbed into his sleigh he called over his shoulder, "We'd better take it one at a time, though."

His friend Mike was not sold on the idea of crossing. In the ice there could be soft spots that had not shown up. Tim's team had to be urged to step into the water. This also gave Mike a few qualms, for animals' instinct usually can be trusted. He watched as his friend's rig made slow progress over the watery trail and was relieved when he saw them draw near the shore. He was about to follow when he heard a loud shout. The hindquarters of the horse on the left had gone through the ice. Leaping from the sleigh, Tim rushed to the head of his team and with the help of the other animal created enough leverage to allow the struggling horse to heave himself out. Tim jumped back on to the sleigh, pulled the team's head sharply to the right, and yelled for them to go.

He was prepared to jump if the sleigh should start to sink through the cracking ice. The first pull was the crucial one, and he was thankful that the sleigh veered far enough to the right that just the back left runner went through for a second. Only a few articles fell into the water and he was able to retrieve most of them. Later, as they sat around the campfire with the freighters discussing the incident, Mike told them that Tim had promised never to risk his team and rig again.

The freighters told my parents that this was the second day they had spent here, and they hoped the ice would freeze enough to allow them to cross into Mirror Landing by the next morning. Realizing they would also have to spend the night on the river, my parents were grateful to accept an invitation for Mother and Carlton to sleep in one of the cabooses.

Next morning Mother and Dad, with Carlton warmly bundled up against the cold, sat quietly in their sleigh watching the activity as they waited their turn to pull out. A group of freighters heading for Athabasca had passed through earlier, informing them that the ice was frozen over except where the horse had gone through, and Tim had marked it with a pole so it was easily seen.

The women had wanted the cabooses parked close together, and now the drivers were having to do a bit of manoeuvering in order to hitch their teams to the vehicles in such close quarters. But nothing could daunt the spirits of these families on such a morning. They were happy to be moving again, and the cold bright air rang to the sound of laughter as the men called out advice and good-natured insults to one another. With more shouts and cracking of whips, the seventeen rigs pulled out.

Most of the families, my parents among them, were stopping in Mirror Landing to buy supplies and enjoy a night's rest in a hotel. The others were heading up Lesser Slave River on the last leg of their journey. Watching them pull away, Mother and Dad once again felt a surge of excitement at being part of this migration.

Babe and Girlie walked briskly up the incline toward Mirror Landing, and Dad noted with pride that their long stride was easily keeping up with the team trotting ahead of them. They seemed none the worse for having spent the night without much shelter, although Dad had risen several times to walk them. The heavy horse blankets he had purchased when he first began freighting, but had seldom used, were worth the price for last night alone.

My parents waved a last goodbye to the Evans family as their caboose rounded a curve in the trail ahead. The Evanses had not hesitated in taking them in last night, even though it meant Mr. Evans had to share a small mattress with my father in the covered space in the back of the sleigh. The caboose was much warmer, but it had been pretty crowded with Mother and Carlton sharing a double mattress with Mrs. Evans and her two children.

Mother had slept next to the six-year-old who had kicked and thrashed until Mother was sure she was black-and-blue. Sleep finally overtook her, but a few hours later the little fellow awoke, crying loudly from a bad dream. They were soon all awake and aware that, in his fright, the laddie had wet the bed. Carlton, disturbed by the noise, woke up and was soon in tears too. Mother tried to reassure him while Mrs. Evans fumbled for matches. She finally got the lamp lit, her child into a dry nightgown, and placed a folded towel over the wet spot. The seven-year-old turned his back on all this, saying in a disgusted voice, "He's always doing this," and was asleep again in a matter of minutes. The others followed his example, but Mother was now wide awake and stayed that way for the rest of the night.

As Mother lay sleepless on the hard mattress, not daring to move for fear of waking the others, she had seen a bright star winking at her through the window. Then the sharp bark of a coyote, followed by its long lonesome cry, had drifted back to her, and she started to compare this life with the one she had left behind in Buffalo. That world was so far away now, she could hardly believe it really existed.

The next morning, Mrs. Evans told Mother her family had been on the trail for nearly a month. While her husband handled the freight sleigh filled with farm implements as well as a few pieces of furniture, she drove the caboose. She was happy they had managed to get the kitchen range inside it.

Mr. Evans had been working as a freighter for the past two years and they had finally saved enough money to start farming. He found good land near Sawridge a year ago and built a cabin and barn. Now he was bringing out his family. It was a story that was becoming familiar to Mother, and she could not help but admire this plucky woman, especially after she confessed there were times she was sure the caboose was about to plunge over the edge of one of the steep hills near Athabasca Landing.

Remembering how quickly Mrs. Evans had fallen asleep, Mother realized how exhausted she must be after driving nearly two hundred miles over winter trails, while coping with two small children.

Mother requested a bath as soon as they arrived at the hotel in Mirror Landing. The wife of the hotel manager had started to refuse her request at first, then, seeing the disappointment in Mother's eyes, relented. She said it would cost them an extra two dollars though, as the water had to be heated on the top of the range. Two stalwart boys lugged up the hot water, filling the oval tub half full. Slipping them each a quarter, Dad asked them to bring two extra pails. When Mother raised her eyebrows at the extravagance, he laughed and said, "But Ollie, their smiles alone were worth it." He teased her when she pulled the crib in front of the tub and draped it with a sheet, saying, "With two such rascals in the room a girl needs some privacy." A soft sigh of contentment escaped from Mother as she eased her tired body into the blissful warmth of the tub.

Carlton soon joined her and she scrubbed him until he was pink and beautiful, then handed him to Dad to dry while she rinsed her hair. Dad lost no time shedding his clothes for his turn at the tub. She put Carlton to bed. The fresh air and warm bath put him quickly to sleep. Mother felt like a young girl again as she snuggled down in the soft bed and listened to her husband's humming as he splashed and scrubbed. Seeing that faraway look in his eyes, she smiled, knowing that he was no longer dreaming of South Africa, but of the adventures ahead. She never would have believed that a small drab room could hold such happiness.

They had been through an ordeal and proved they could take it along with other northerners. With two-thirds of their journey behind them, she was not worried about the last hundred miles.

Dad finished his bath and they were soon sound asleep.

Mother woke to Carlton's demands to be taken up out of the crib. Dad had already left to attend the horses. They had decided to let the team rest a day before starting on the last part of their trip. Mother did some necessary washing and repacking, but took time to walk through the little town with Dad and Carlton.

They found a bakery-tea shop and were delighted to try out the delicious pastries and buns. It was exactly the kind of lunch a one and a half year old boy liked best and seldom got, and his parents enjoyed it as much as he did. Before leaving the shop, Mother put in a large order for fresh bread to take with them the next morning.

The trip up the winding river from Mirror Landing was a disappointment to my father; he failed to see signs of the good farm land he had heard about. There was only bush, mostly poplar and birch, and the only sign of life was an old rabbit that crossed their path. The sun disappeared and the grey light filtering through the clouds revealed a landscape caught in the hard, uncrackable grip of winter. Seeing a clearing ahead, they imagined a barn with fields and other buildings such as they had seen along the Athabasca route. They were not prepared for the bleak scene that met their eyes.

A small cabin, icicles nearly as big as elephant tusks hanging from its eaves, looked quite deserted. Snow had piled up nearly to the window, and there was only a thin spiral of smoke drifting from a tin stovepipe to tell them the place was inhabited. A short distance from the cabin was a barn. A small shed leaned against it but there were no signs of animals. As they rounded a bend and looked back, they saw, just beyond the small fields, a plot with two wooden crosses. They looked at each other, knowing that in the spring the fields would turn green once more.

The trail continued to wind along the banks of the river. Every now and then they caught a glimpse of wood cut and piled beside the river banks, fuel for the hungry furnaces of the steamboats that would soon be plying these waters again. The woodcutters, mostly homesteaders, took advantage of the new industry to earn extra cash during the slack season. One of them, Bill Burns, was a local hero and ex-prize fighter who had once been friends with the famous John L. Sullivan. Burns was also a prankster whose exploits were a never-ending topic of discussion locally. Burns had taken up homesteading two years ago near Soto, but preferred spending his evenings in the livelier town of Mirror Landing.

James G. MacGregor, who wrote about Alberta's early days, tells this story about one of Bill's favourite areas in his book, *Land of Twelve Foot Davis:*

> As the settlers unavailingly urged their placid
> oxen to hurry over the water-covered meadows
> on the south trail, many a squall of rain
> descended upon them from out of the Swan
> Hills to the south. Seen from the lake, these
> hills, comprised of House Mountain, Deer
> Mountain and Wallace Mountain, appear as a
> low tableland. In the lore of the Indians these
> mountains are the home of the thunder. In them
> dwell many enormous birds. Now and again
> they flap their wings with a loud noise and this
> is what men call thunder. These giant birds
> never molest men, although, of course, it would
> be tempting fate to try to visit them or see them;
> since they never leave their favorite abode, no
> one has ever seen them. In 1898, white men
> built the old Swan River Trail. Though they did
> not see the thunder birds, their road availed
> them little and was soon abandoned. White
> men sometimes rush in where Indians fear to
> tread.

Bill Burns also had a tale about how he almost lost his life in the haunt of the thunderbirds. It happened while he was working with a team of surveyors who were running the eighteenth baseline over Wallace Mountain. One day, when Bill and another man named Ed Larue were returning to a former campsite, they came upon the tracks of a huge bear, who often fed on the dump of a former camp. They followed the tracks to the dump and decided to set a snare for the animal. They worked all afternoon rigging up a snare that, if the animal took the bait, would jerk him off his feet and strangle him.

The next morning they returned to see if the snare had caught anything. It had. As Bill, the only man with a gun, peered over the crest of the steep hill leading to the trap, he was frozen in his track by what he declared to have been the most blood-curdling roar he had ever heard. There, less than a hundred feet from where he stood, was a huge grizzly. But the snare of three-quarter-inch rope had passed over the bear's shoulders and clinched around his hind quarters so that his back feet were lifted about a foot off the ground.

The bear had made good use of his front feet, though, and his jaws as well. Bill said the trees and bush for ten feet around were ripped and torn and beaten to shreds. Saplings three and four inches in diameter had been snapped like toothpicks, and the bear had "sawed" huge chunks off the tree that held him captive.

Bill was rooted to the spot in fear, but he had the gun; it was up to him to kill the bear. The first shot, declared Bill, caught the bear somewhere in the ribs, but only caused a slight hesitation in his rantings and roarings. The second shot had more effect – both on Bill and the bear – it cut the rope that held the animal and he immediately made straight for Bill. Fortunately, the old boxer had time to get in another shot. This caught the bear in the eye and he dropped in his tracks about ten feet from the muzzle of the gun. Bill dropped in his tracks too but he said it was only from fatigue.

CHAPTER EIGHT

Porcupine Stew

The whiteness of the snow and ice stretched ahead in an endless expanse, relieved only by the dark shape of Dog Island to the west.

This frozen expanse was Lesser Slave Lake, my parents' goal for several weeks. As they contemplated it their carefree bantering ended. They had been told winter travel across this lake could be dangerous but they had not been too concerned. Now as they gazed across its vast snowy surface they felt alarm, particularly Mother. She thought of the "safe" little rivers they had left behind, forgetting the times of hardship and near tragedy they and other travellers had endured along their shores. Telling herself she was worrying needlessly, she turned to Carlton who was playing with the small wooden sleigh they had bought him before leaving Sawridge, and shared a smile with Dad as they watched him push it up and down the back of the seat.

Dad, sensing Mother's uneasiness, decided to tell her how ice ridges are formed on the lake. The ridges are composed of thick jagged ice several feet high. Their light blue colour reflects the clear water beneath them. They usually extend for miles in a curving line across these big northern lakes and are caused by the ice shrinking during cold nights. The shrinking causes cracks two to three feet wide to open. Then, as the sun's heat expands the ice, it moves back together again. If the ice expands beyond its original size it overlaps and often piles up twenty feet or higher, forming the ridges.

John Denison, in Edith Iglauer's book, *Denison's Ice Road* (New York: E. P. Dutton, 1975), gives this account: "Jimmy was sitting in the back of a caboose once on Great Bear Lake. . . when the ice heaved straight up about a mile away from him . . . . It was in the spring, and he said it was like an earthquake, with everything shakin', and heaving.' There was a great loud bang like a bomb, combined with a heavy thud when the ice cracked. For a second he said he did not know where to run, until he realized what had happened." [pp.231-232]

A phenomenon such as this must occur every year on Lesser Slave Lake where the pressure ridges often rise up to ten feet; and it is quite possible that few have ever witnessed the formation of one. In fact, Jimmy Watson's experience of actually seeing this happen on Great Bear Lake is a rare one, as this driver relates.

"Del Curry [an old friend of Denison's] says the most frustratin' experience he ever had was being on a pressure ridge on Great Slave Lake while it was forming. Guess why? He was asleep. He was in a Bombardier, and had turned around to wait for the man behind him and Del could feel his vehicle shakin' and tremblin', and thought in his sleep that it was the other guy bumpin' him to wake him up. When he opened his eyes, there was a pressure ridge eight feet high right in front of his eyes. . . and he had slept right through it. . . ." [p. 232]

Edith Iglauer writes, "Of all the distinctive features of the northern weather that men who constantly deal with ice dread, they fear the pressure ridge the most, even while it fascinates them; treacherous, deceptive, dangerous, frequently impassable." [p. 281]

Iglauer knew this danger personally, for she was travelling with Denison on Great Bear Lake when Fud, his big thirty-six foot truck, nearly fell into the icy black water. Yet she had the courage to return the following year and travel 1,275 miles in order to record the story of this man's speciality in building ice roads where no one else had dared to make them.

The unique road constructed over snow and ice, known as

Denison's Road, is an overland link between two of the world's largest inland seas – Great Slave Lake, whose southern border is one hundred miles north of the Alberta boundary, and Great Bear Lake on the Arctic Circle.

Iglauer travelled night and day with Denison and his road crew, contending with the savage cold and blinding blizzards, at times with one hand on the door handle, ready to leap from the truck, at other times braced against the dashboard to keep from crashing through the windshield as Denison sped over the rough terrain. She learned to drive his huge trucks and often held a heater to the windshield of old Fud to ensure clear vision for the driver. She also helped with the cooking and other chores as she listened to hair-raising tales of the crew's adventures. She learned that at temperatures of sixty below, steel cables could snap and that trucks and other vehicles must be kept running night and day.

Dad, who lived to the age of ninety-four, spent his winters in Guadalajara, Mexico, and his summers in Peace River during his later years, would have been fascinated by Ms. Iglauer's book describing the high-powered equipment and techniques now used in constructing an ice road. He often used to say he had lived to see it all – from the horse-and-buggy age to the atomic age, and he was as excited as his grandchildren as he watched the first man walk on the moon.

Dad had not been aware of the danger of these "live ridges," as they are called, until the night they arrived at Sawridge. While unharnessing his team he noticed a small wooden bridge in a freighter's sleigh and was told it was used to span the cracks before attempting a crossing. The man then went on to say he hoped the ice would remain safe for a while because cutting through the tough ridges was a backbreaking job, usually requiring four men armed with axes. Once a passage had been chopped through, the ice was tested by leading an old horse across the opening. If the freighters were still uneasy, they attached a logging chain to the sleigh and the horse dragged it slowly through the gap. Thus assured, they hitched up the team and went on to the next ridge.

The following account from *Denison's Ice Road* as related

by John Denison's nephew and crew member, Jimmy Watson, shows that the intrepid road builder also had to take chances to get his supplies through:

John's got a certain way of asking you to do things so you can't refuse. . . .

I remember once we were coming south after the northern operations were finished for that year, driving vehicles loaded with equipment. I was carrying a truck and John's TD-14 International tractor on my highboy and we were crossing the Mackenzie River on the bridge at Fort Providence. It was early May, and the load limit in the spring was fifteen thousand pounds. Well, the truck itself probably weighed thirty thousand pounds, and I had more like one hundred thousand altogether, but John said, 'Take her the way she is.' I was sure I'd have to change my underwear after I crossed, and I knew I was a little bit nervous, but subconsciously I was damned scared. After all, when you know you've got way too much of a load maybe you don't show it, but you know it. Well, I took the dumb thing across the Mackenzie on the ice bridge, and the ice shook a little bit and lots of water came up. It seems a lot longer when you're driving like that but it's only about two miles, and about forty feet deep in the deepest spot. The ice was very spongy and sort of sank but it was okay. When I got to the other side I had to change loads with another truck driver. He took my load south and the next morning I took his north, forty-two-thousand pounds of groceries. We just switched trailers, because my truck had six-wheel drive and his didn't. During the night, the government pulled the chain across the ice bridge and put a padlock on it so nobody could cross anymore that season. Del Curry was at the south side of the bridge with us too, with a gravel truck to drive north and he took a crescent wrench and undid the bolt, unfastening the chain between the posts. We proceeded to go across, with Del first, in the gravel truck, just hoping there was enough ice under the overflow water that was all over the road, covering the top and cracks and holes, some of which were four feet deep. You'd fall into the odd hole, but with six-wheel drive you can pull yourself out... one hole was *really* deep and I remember the van tipping. It had me quite nervous.[pp. 68-69]

Wherever my parents stopped, they met with friendly people anxious to inform them of historical sites and interesting stories about the area through which they were passing. This is how they knew they were passing Dog Island, located about two miles out on the lake to the west of Sawridge. It was on this island, the largest on the lake, that the Hudson's Bay Company had built a trading post over 185 years ago. Thirty-five years later, the North West Trading Company built a fort along the southern shore of the lake, not far from the island.

Winter transportation was difficult in those days as horses had not yet been brought into the country and dog teams were used to pull loads of up to four hundred pounds. The North West Company started a fishery on the island as there was an abundance of fish of several varieties. These thrifty Scots and French found that the fish, when smoked and dried, were an economical food for the hordes of dogs they kept, and for themselves. This is how Dog Island acquired its name.

My parents also learned that the inhabitants of this island, Captain Herman Nicklas and his wife, now lived on the island and were in the process of building a sumptuous lodge that would cause Dog Island to become something of a social center, with formal teas and summer picnics for visitors. He and a partner, Jim Cromwell, had set up a smokehouse on the island a few years previously, as well as a lumber mill which they ran for a short while.

Nicklas was a German who had earned his master's papers on a windjammer that sailed between Germany and the Cameroons. He survived a shipwreck off Chile and mutiny in the South Seas. After emigrating to Canada, he homesteaded in Saskatchewan, where he and his wife nearly starved. They moved to Edmonton where they met Jim Crowell, who hired Nicklas to command the *Northern Light* on Lesser Slave Lake. Nicklas was soon to discover that storms and mutiny could occur on Lesser Slave Lake just as on the high seas. One time, he was headed west, about four miles past Dog Island, when a terrific storm blew up. His cargo of telegraph wires and insulators was all dead weight. He tried to turn and get into the lee of the island, but the boat got caught in a deep trough and, being a sidewheeler, could not get out. The captain was having a tough time keeping her from being swamped, as the wild winds tossed the hundred-and-twenty-foot vessel from side to side.

Realizing he had to lighten the load, Nicklas yelled for the deck hands and the survey crew he had aboard to start throwing the heavy stuff over the side. Fearing for their lives the men became hysterical. They rushed to the wheelhouse and told the captain they were taking charge as he did not know his job.

Nicklas let out a blast, telling them he would not be dictated to and that this was not the first vessel he had commanded. The two women aboard, Mrs. Nicklas and a surveyor's wife, saved the situation by remaining cool and stating they did not see any great danger. This had a calming effect on the men, as well as on the captain. He soon had them throwing the heavy freight overboard and got the *Northern Light* out of the trough.

Looking at the small island, Mother and Dad tried to imagine wild waves lashing its shores. All was white now with snow everywhere; drifts several feet high covered the ice as if a blanket had formed a border along the packed, darkened trail. It was early morning and the sky was a soft pinkish grey backdrop against the low hills sprinkled with black, scrubby trees.

Their route followed the south shore road until it reached

the Narrows, the halfway point of the lake, then cut across its narrow waist to the north shore and proceeded west to Shaw's Point. Grouard was just another four or five miles beyond that. The trail led past stopping places located close to sites where fur traders had constructed their posts to trade with the local Indians.

The long, straight ice road would soon be turning landwards toward one of these stopping houses where they planned to have their lunch and then cross the Narrows. Dad's keen eyes had not been playing tricks on him; they were approaching one of these places now. It was a stopping place Mother would always remember, for it was here she was tricked into eating porcupine stew.

A large number of people had gathered at the trading post as the day was warm and sunny. My parents guessed correctly that they had come for supplies while the ice was still solid. Drawing closer they could see that several Indian trappers had arrived, their dogs pulling sleighs piled high with their winter catch of fur. Mother and Dad smiled at each other remembering the *moochigan* they had witnessed their first night out of Athabasca, and knew that the moccasin telegraph had been active. Mother asked Dad to pull over, but when she got close to the furs nothing was visible but the shiny skins and bushy tails of the fox pelts, for they had been turned inside out.

The fur trader, a tall well-built man, came out to meet them and introduced himself as Robbie McFee. His reply to Dad's comment that he detected a trace of Scots burr in his voice was that his father was a Scot who had been with the North West Trading Company and married a woman from the Cree tribe. Noticing Mother's interest in the beaver pelt he held in his hands, he handed it to her for a closer look saying it was an exceptionally fine one. He demonstrated how to judge a prime fur by running his fingers through the thick, luxurious beaver skin. My parents marvelled as he told them that although the beaver spent virtually his entire life in the water not a drop penetrated the animal's thick fur. Mr. McFee surprised Mother by saying he bet she owned a beaver hat. She did, although she had never related it to this fur. (She made it into a bonnet for me many years later, when it went out of style.) Imitating his mother, Carlton ran his fingers through the soft fur, then asked, "Where's Brownie?"

My parents asked how far the trappers had travelled this day and were told that most of them were from around Big Point on the Narrows. Mr. McFee explained that it was the largest Indian colony on the lake. When Dad asked which pelts brought the best prices he was surprised to learn that the traders dealt mostly in beaver, martin, fisher and otter, the prices ranging in that order, and beaver topped the price list considerably. Weasel, famous for trimming the robes of royalty, was practically worthless as was coyote, fox, and wolf.

Dad broke off the conversation saying they would never get any lunch at that rate, although he had enjoyed learning first-hand something of the fur trade. Mr. McFee laughed and said, "Never fear; my wife runs the stopping house and is also the cook. She's of French-Cree extraction and not a Scot like myself – there will be plenty of food!"

Dad was back from the stables before Mother had time to take Carlton's heavy clothes off, saying their host had sent his boys to tend to the team and all he had to do was measure out the oats.

Mother was starting to ladle a helping of stew onto her plate; but when told it was rabbit, looked appealingly at Dad and quickly passed the dish to him. An older man who was just finishing his meal came to her rescue and asked if she liked pork stew. Too embarrassed to answer, she nodded and he slipped into the kitchen and was soon back saying all was well as there was enough left for her. In answer to her grateful smile he leaned across the table and said quietly that he hoped he'd never have to eat rabbit again himself.

Mother was starving and ate two helpings of the stew. On her way out she complimented Mrs. McFee, saying she had never tasted such good pork stew, and that she could almost have taken it for chicken. The attractive dark woman looked a little puzzled and answered she was glad Mother had enjoyed it.

It was then her daughter let the cat out of the bag saying, "That wasn't pork, that was porcupine." Mother was too astonished to say a word, but the old trapper and Mrs. McFee looked so embarrassed that she burst out laughing and the others joined in, including Carlton.

It was dark long before they reached the next stopping house but the good weather held. As they gazed at the white earth and black heavens filled with twinkling stars, they felt part of it and were content.

CHAPTER NINE

The Storm

A week beyond the Indian village of Big Point and nearly across the lake, Mother and Dad anticipated their journey's end. The trail over the lake was smooth and straight and they made good progress. With a greater distance between stopping houses, they had pushed on through long days. These were days for thoughts about the trail, the long road they had endured, and the uncertain future that lay at its end.

Grouard, Dad believed, could double its size of 3,500 people within a year of the railway's arrival. Business would be good and perhaps they could recoup some of their financial losses. "Thirty-five hundred people!" Mother exclaimed. "It will seem like a city compared to the Indian camps and villages. And I didn't think Edmonton seemed much compared to Buffalo." Dad laughed and after a moment's pause asked how she felt about the possibility of living on a farm. Mother was thoughtful for a while. She knew nothing about farming, but she knew something about people, and she recalled the Andrews who came from Edmonton but were now happily involved with life on the land. "It might," she began carefully, "be a better way of life for our family than managing a restaurant and hotel." There was a long silence. Then, turning toward Dad, she was startled by the look of amazement and admiration in his eyes. To hide her self-consciousness she said a bit defensively, "If you'd been around more those last few months in Edmonton you might have noticed how much I disliked the hotel business. Having to serve meals may be more than we can cope with." Dad secretly agreed with her, but not wanting to admit it, he reminded her that her mother would soon be joining them and could help out. Mother, however, had her own opinion about this.

They were so engrossed in their discussion, they failed to notice until then that the sky had turned a metallic grey. The sun was dull and remote making everything seem still and lifeless. Mother was reminded of the eerie feeling they had experienced the night before as they gazed at the phenomenon of the full moon – as if they were looking inside a great circle of light with a deep black well at the exact centre of which floated the bright round moon. The sky seemed to haze over, dulling the stars, while the moon stared down at them from its black space, holding them spellbound. Dad had told Mother that such a sky could portend a storm. They both remembered this as they watched ominous dark clouds gather on the horizon. Suddenly, great tides of wind drove down on them – screaming winds that chilled the marrow and congealed the blood. The first blast caught them unprepared, and they dived under the buffalo robe, awakening Carlton who let out loud cries. Mother pulled him closer in an effort to comfort him.

The team seemed to falter. In a flash, Dad tightened the reins and was steadying them. Girlie was getting the worst of it. The north wind was hitting them head on, but great gusts were also driving in from the west catching her in the flank. Dad was blinded by the wind lashing furiously across the lake and whipping the snow into needles of ice. Mother hastily wound a wool scarf around her head and face and tucked Carlton under the robe. A gust caught the sleigh sideways, shoving it across the trail and into a snowbank, bringing the horses to a floundering halt. The force of impact knocked Dad out of his seat against Mother so hard she was nearly sent over the side. She felt bruised and shaken but not seriously hurt. Carlton cried out in fright.

Dad started to get out to see how badly they were stuck. He

realized he needed his isinglass goggles to protect his eyes from the sharp needles of wind-driven ice. Mother did not need goggles to see that their situation was serious and she shivered, knowing they could freeze to death if they did not find shelter soon. While Dad was adjusting his goggles, she noticed blood oozing from several tiny cuts on his face. He shrugged off her alarm but did not refuse the scarf she was trying to tie around his fur collar in the driving wind. She was having difficulties between the force of the wind and Dad's impatience to see to his team.

He was relieved that they seemed to have escaped damage. He was worried though, and hoped Mother had not noticed. His confidence returned as he picked up the reins and, shouting encouragement to the team, slapped them across the rumps. This was the time for Babe and Girlie to prove their worth. They did not let him down. Bowing their heads against the icy blast, they dug in and with a mighty heave had them out of the drift and on the trail again.

Their progress was slow but steady for the next few miles, but the wind was gaining momentum, flinging great hills of snow in their path. These were not ordinary drifts, but promontories five or six feet high and up to twelve feet across that froze almost the instant the wind dumped them. The trail was almost obliterated now, the horses dim and shadowy figures. This was a whiteout – a weather condition northerners fear most – when strong winds combine with heavy snowfall to create a thick swirl that reduces visibility to zero. It is similar to navigating through a cloud – everything is blank. Mother envied the wild animals, wishing they too could burrow beneath the snow and sleep until it was all over.

Nothing could keep out the biting cold. The wind found its way into the lower part of the sleigh-box. Even though Mother's feet were resting on one of the warm boulders she had had the foresight to heat the evening before, she was very cold, especially on her left side. After a time she asked Dad how he was making out. He just shook his head, and she realized his lips were stiff from cold making it difficult to answer. She told him his nose and cheeks were turning white again and he stopped the team for a rest. They needed it, and he had to warm his hands, fearing they might be frozen. Lowering his cold body under the buffalo robe, he asked mother to help pull off his mitts.

She could tell from his expression that he was suffering intense pain. Thrusting his curd-white fingers against his body he groaned as the blood began to circulate. At the same time he assured Mother that they were not really frozen.

Mother offered to drive and watch for ice ridges to give Dad a chance to thaw out. She was so brave but he was too worried to stay under the heavy robe for long. As ridges appeared a uniform distance apart one should show up anytime now, and it would be hard to see in a storm like this. He also knew that the team could not keep going much longer. If they played out before the next ridge they would be in a serious predicament.

A sudden gust lifted the curtain of snow to reveal a long ridge of ice, about ten feet high, beyond the snowbanks that hung over the trail. Dad stopped the team, hopeful that the worst was almost over, if only he could get the rig across the snow bank into the shelter of the ridge. With great difficulty in the tearing wind, he covered Babe and Girlie with their blankets.

But there would be no rest for him until he mowed down the hard snowbank. Armed with his axe, he gave it all he had but he did not make much headway. His hands were in no condition for this work. In desperation he kicked the hard snow with his heavy boots and was able to break down the frozen bank enough to manoeuver the team and sleigh into the shelter of the ice ridge. Amazingly, they were almost completely sheltered between the ridge and a huge snow drift. Except for a fine spray of powdered snow swirling around them and the sound of the wind shrieking over their heads, they could hardly believe the fierceness of the storm still existed.

Dad unhitched the team and tied them to the back of the sleigh. They knickered softly when they smelled oats. Commandeering the bale of hay Sam had given Mother for a footstool before they left Edmonton, he ripped it open and fed half to the team, saving a few handfuls for starting a fire. Mother watched a bit wistfully; the team deserved the extra rations, but she would miss her comfortable footrest.

Dad soon had a fire going, the four boulders and grill in place, and kept an eye on a pan of snow to make sure it did not scorch before melting down a bit. Mother offered to help, but he told her he was not taking any chances on having to deliver their second child on the lake. She looked so small and vulnerable; he blamed himself for not heeding warnings about crossing the lake alone. He realized she was praying as she lay, eyes closed, with a pillow under her head and the buffalo robe over her on the wide sleigh seat. Carlton, wrapped in his quilt, sat on the other half of the seat and munched a cookie while he watch his dad slice bacon and toast bread for their supper. The wild storm could not get at them now.

Lulled by the occasional snorting and whooshing noises of the horses as they tore and munched their hay, Mother fell into a deep sleep. Dad had to waken her when it was time to eat and when she murmured she was too tired, persuaded her that she needed to replenish body heat. Later, after putting her to bed in the back of the sleigh beside Carlton, he crawled in beside them and, in words we so often heard him use, was "out like a light."

Mother wakened with a start. She sat up, wondering where she was and what had startled her. It was very still and dark and she seemed to be fully dressed. She thought she must be dreaming. Then she heard once more the startled snorting of Babe and Girlie, and felt the jolt of the sleigh as they jumped aside.

Dad was awake now too and investigating what had frightened his team. It was then he saw the wolf. Calling softly to Mother he pointed the animal out to her while pulling on his boots. His first concern was to calm the team. He unfastened their ropes so that if they spooked they would not upset the sleigh. He spoke to them in a low, soothing voice as he clung to their leads. "Easy Babe. Whoa, Girlie. Settle down my beauties," he said quietly, as he let them move back a few paces. He heaved a sigh of relief when they settled down.

The wolf was too occupied by licking up the remains of last night's supper to pay them much attention. In the bright moonlight, he looked like a huge silver dog. Startled suddenly, he looked straight at Mother, his luminous eyes blazing. A strange feeling rippled through her. She remembered the moonlit night when they had been so thrilled by the wolves' wild music. The wolf continued to stare at them with a curious expression in his slanted eyes. In the light of the full moon, his grey, angular face was highlighted with touches of black and amber, his upright inquisitive ears framed by a matching ruff. Then he started to walk away and, with a nonchalant glance over his shoulder, seemed to grin at them with his long pointed muzzle and white jagged teeth. Seconds later he was gone, a silver wraith melting into the moonlit shadows of the ice ridge.

Mother shook her head, wondering if she had really seen him that plainly, or if he might have been only half-wolf like Joseph's lead dog. She told Dad she could not understand the animal's fearlessness. He commented that a wolf's pelt was of so little value the trappers usually left them in peace. Mother smiled at this. She felt that their meeting with the wolf was a good omen, sent to let them know they had nothing to fear.

It was five A.M. by Dad's big watch as he settled the team with the rest of the hay. He guessed it could not be more than ten miles to Shaw's Point, and from there just another five or six miles to Grouard. The wind dropped. The northern air was clear and exhilarating, but breaking a trail after the heavy snowstorm would be as hard a task as anything they could put a team through. The drifts whipped up by the wind would settle to about one-third their original height in twenty-four hours. If they left now they would be up to the horses' knees in snow most of the way. Dad looked out at Babe and Girlie. They stood quietly and he knew they needed more time to rest. Mother's face was pale and drawn from the strain of yesterday's ordeal and now that the excitement was over he realized that he was very tired as well. They ate some cookies to stave off hunger pangs then crawled back into the sleigh, content to sleep for a few more hours. Dad had hopes that someone else, anxious to get through, would break trail for them.

The sun coming up over the horizon awakened my parents from their exhausted sleep. They opened their eyes to a world that sparkled with diamonds, as sunbeams caught the curving ice-ridge. For a moment they sat mesmerized by its beauty, until a thought hit them – in a few hours they would be across the lake, and Grouard just a few miles beyond.

Dad fed the team and prepared a meagre breakfast of toast and coffee while Mother changed Carlton and tidied herself as best she could. Having slept in her clothes, it did not take her long. The cold was less intense, the azure sky swept clean by the storm, and the lake stretched out in a vast sheet of unbroken white. After a struggle to get the rig back on the trail, they resumed their journey. In places the drifts reached almost to the horses' bellies and the going was tough. But Babe and Girlie seemed to sense that their gruelling journey was nearing an end, as they snorted and bobbed heads playfully before they settled down and carefully placed their hind feet in holes made by their forefeet.

Resting them frequently, Dad stopped in mid-morning to feed his team a half-measure of oats. He fussed over and talked to them as he rubbed them down with a rough gunnysack. The air had warmed considerably. Tired of sitting, Mother decided to take advantage of the break and take her little one for a walk; but walking turned out to be impossible in the deep snow, especially for Carlton's short legs. However, she soon had him laughing as they tossed snow at one another. They were having such fun, Dad thought it a shame to break it up. Playfully he tossed a snowball at them before scooping Carlton up with one arm and half-carrying Mother to the sleigh with the other. Tired but refreshed after their little burst of energy, they were only too glad to be assisted.

Lulled by the jingle of the harness and the warm sun, sleep overcame Mother and Carlton. Dad too was unable to keep his eyes open; he wound the reins around the post and drifted off. He dozed until he became aware in his subconscious state that the horses were no longer struggling through deep snow. The unpredictable warmth of the sun had melted and packed the drifts enough to support the team's weight, and this speeded them considerably.

The trail followed the north shore and snaked around a broad curve that brought them within sight of a poplar grove. After the barren waste of the lake it was a welcome scene. They gazed at the tall trees whose mantles of melting snow thrust toward the blue sky and perfumed the air with the pungent odour of running sap. They heard a pair of woodpeckers and caught an occasional glimpse of the birds' bright heads flashing from tree to tree.

The smell of woodsmoke and barking of dogs told them that they were approaching Shaw's Point, much to Dad's surprise, as he thought it was still an hour's distance away. Before long they caught sight of the Hudson's Bay Company warehouse and a cluster of several smaller buildings. Shaw's Point had been named for Angus Shaw, who had built the first Hudson's Bay trading post here nearly one hundred years ago. The main post had been moved nearer to Grouard and was replaced by the big warehouse. As the sleigh pulled up the incline, it was met by a group of people curious to see how this outfit, the first to get through, had weathered the storm. Two freighters who intended to head south in the morning were especially interested.

Stepping forward as Dad pulled up, the freighters carefully noted the good condition of the big Clydesdales. They were amazed to find a woman and a child in the rig. Dad admitted that they should have left earlier with his partner, but he had no idea that storms on the lake could be so severe. He was a bit embarrassed as he admitted that he had needed his wife's help – she had driven through the worst of the storm until he was able to get the circulation going in his frostbitten hands. "I'll never complain that my team is slow again," he said. "They dug in and pulled us out with a mighty heave, when I thought we were hopelessly stuck."

These men had been through bad storms, but never without the help of a back-up rig. They now looked at these "greenhorns" with respect and offered to help. One undertook to stable and feed the team while his partner helped Mother and

Carlton out of the sleigh. On their feet, my parents found they could barely navigate, so great was their exhaustion after weeks of travel and yesterday's storm. It was not long before these friendly freighters persuaded my parents to take advantage of the comfortable rooming house at Shaw's Point.

My parents arrived at a time when these men were feeling "bushed" after a long winter – being cooped up while waiting out the storm had not helped matters. They did not exactly know why they were intrigued by the young couple. Mother was pretty enough to win their admiration, and she really made a hit with her friendliness toward the local women, but it was to my father that their eyes turned most often. There was something about him – a certain aura – giving the impression that he had recently come from distant places. Wanting to learn more about his past, they invited my parents to join them that evening.

After a light lunch, Dad and Carlton, trailing behind with his bag of toys, made their way to the parlour where Dad had earlier spotted a pile of Edmonton *Bulletin* newspapers. While he browsed through them, the baby played happily, giving Mother a chance for a rest and a bath. After supper that evening, she and Dad joined the freighters and their friends in the parlour.

My parents enjoyed meeting these men. Ninety percent of them were freighting to put aside enough money to get started on the land, or had already taken out a homestead and needed cash to keep it going. The fee for filing on a homestead was ten dollars. This was forfeited if a homesteader did not stick it out for three years in order to prove it up and get title to the land. A grim jest among settlers was that when the going got tough, the government bet you a quarter section against ten dollars that you could not stick it out for three years. However, the men at Shaw's Point that night wore looks of determination on their weather-beaten faces. Nearly three-quarters of a century have passed since that evening, and most of those people did stick it out. Many of their children and grandchildren are still on the farms, reaping the benefits of the land those early settlers worked so hard to claim.

The men were puzzled to learn that Dad was born in

Illinois. One freighter asked where he had acquired his English accent. Dad, glad to forget for a moment his worries over the hotel, told them the highlights of his South African experiences. Mother watched him, eyes shining, happy to see him in a carefree mood again. Leaning toward him, she suggested he tell his snake story. Later he was to tell and retell this story to his children, and we never tired of listening to it:

Because of their knowledge of the South African countryside, Dad and Frederick were able to enlist as scouts at the outbreak of the Boer War. One particular day, they had travelled deep into bushland to locate an enemy camp and they had an uncanny feeling the enemy was not far away. Tethering their mounts, they cautiously made their way to the top of a steep hill, crawling on their bellies for the last few yards.

Their hunch proved right. A platoon of Boers was approaching the hill. The pair made their way back to the horses, mounted them and rode into the jungle, travelling as quickly as possible and keeping an eye out for snakes in the branches of trees above them. By the time they were far enough from the main road, darkness had descended. Finding a small clearing, they tethered and fed their horses, and after a frugal meal wrapped themselves in blankets. Using their saddles for pillows, the two were soon asleep.

Towards morning, my Dad's sixth sense cautioned him to be very still. He could not account for the icy feeling that crept over him. Overhead, the grey light of dawn was beginning to filter through the branches and he was able to make out the vague shapes of the horses. Wide awake now, he felt a clammy coldness pressing against his back, and looked over his shoulder. A huge boa constrictor curled between him and Frederick. Terror filled his heart. He told himself to calm down. A sudden movement could awaken the reptile whose natural instincts could make an end to them both. He inched slowly away, then rolled gently over until he was free of the snake. He crept around to the other side and, placing his hand over Frederick's mouth, whispered for him to move with caution. After one look, he complied. They were able to slip away leading their horses, leaving their saddles behind. They decided they would rather ride bareback than confront that huge reptile. After several days they made it back to camp.

The snake, Dad said, had probably made a kill earlier and curled between them for warmth. Unless startled, he was quite harmless until he became hungry again. They fully intended to return for their saddles but the more they thought about it, the more they became convinced that they would never find the clearing. They were finally issued new saddles. The company commander said that he preferred live cowards to dead heroes, especially as scouts were at a premium.

When Dad finished his story, he admitted that he should have preferred telling an African experience that gave him a little more stature but that his wife, however, seemed to prefer this one. On this note of levity, the party broke up. My parents went to their room feeling like celebrities, with everyone wishing them well and telling them how much they had enjoyed hearing Dad's tales.

CHAPTER TEN

Grouard Grows

Early the next morning Dad quietly slipped out of the rooming house, leaving the other two asleep, and walked over the sparkling snow to the barn to groom his team. Noticing a change in weather, he felt his impatience vanish as he breathed in the balmy air.

Whistling softly, Dad felt time stand still as he brushed the horses and wondered what the future might hold in this new land. Thinking of their last day on the lake brought to his mind the story of how this beautiful Lesser Slave Lake had been given its name.

Slavey was the name of an Indian tribe that lived along the shores of the lake until driven further west by their fierce enemies, the Cree. When white traders came to this area and asked the Cree who the vanquished tribe were, they were told they were the Slaves, a tribe of little importance. But, two vast lakes and a mighty river would be known until the end of time as Great Slave Lake, Lesser Slave Lake, and Slave River. When traders finally encountered this band and asked their name, the Indians said, "We are the Dene – the people."

Stirring in her comfortable bed, Mother felt rested and ready for the last leg of their journey. Later, leading Carlton to where Dad was hitching the team to the sleigh, she remarked how shipshape everything looked. Dad was pleased that she had noticed the leather and polished brass he had been working on for the past two hours. He was especially pleased with the team's dappled coats. They fairly gleamed in the morning sun. Dad looked at Mother to see if she was as excited as he. When their eyes met, they laughed. Then, raising their arms, they startled their little son with the cry, "Yea, Grouard at last!" Then they were off.

As they followed the shoreline, they noticed buildings and realized that Shaw's Point and the outer district of Grouard were beginning to merge. They watched around every curve for signs of the town, and were excited to see the Hudson's Bay trading post up ahead. Their journey was almost over!

Looking over the solid old trading post buildings, with their green roofs and freshly whitewashed log walls, they thought them very picturesque against the backdrop of the snow-covered bay. In front of one building, Mother noticed a wooden press used to flatten furs for shipping. A short distance away stood the Royal Northwest Mounted Police barracks and district headquarters. Two young constables, exercising their mounts, cantered over to greet my parents. They looked very trim in their neat uniforms. They saluted my father in a dignified way but showed their youthful exuberance by flashing my pretty mother appreciative smiles. When Dad asked the young officers how they had known they were new arrivals, one of them laughed, and nodded towards Babe and Girlie, saying, "There's not a team to match this one in the whole Peace River county."

My parents drove on to a wooden bridge that spanned the narrows at the eastern end of town, near Willow Creek. The bridge, built in 1907, was then the longest of its kind in Alberta. From a distance they caught sight of the Catholic mission, St. Antoine's, the second oldest in the Peace River district. A staff of thirty-two nuns and priests were teaching hundreds of Native children to read and write English. The mission also had a hospital with dental care and operated a sawmill. The white buildings, beautifully situated against a forest of dark pines, stood out in stark relief against the snowy brow of the hill. Below, the frozen lakeshore curved into the distance.

Years earlier, in 1883, Father Grouard, who gave his name to the town by the lake, visited Father Caligan at the original mission on the lakeshore. Impressed by the beauty of the site, he vowed to return and rebuild the mission and later made good his promise.

The town of Grouard, then called Lesser Slave Lake, began life as a Hudson's Bay trading post whose only competitor was Deome Desjarlais, a Métis, who claimed to be the area's first trader and general store owner. Later, the town became the terminus of the steamboat route from Athabasca Landing. Goldseekers travelling to the Klondike caused it to grow in size and importance.

My parents could soon see the main street of Grouard. It stretched below them in a long straight line between the hill and the neck of frozen water leading to the bay. Hemmed in by the lake and the dense forest, the early settlers built their places of business along the narrow flat with their homes behind them.

With a flick of Dad's whip, Babe and Girlie entered Grouard at a fast trot. The town was booming. Even on its outskirts there was an expectancy in the air, as the sound of hammer and saw broke the stillness. Further up the street, the framework of two-storeyed buildings stood out against the sky.

Ignoring the state of the street, Dad whistled cheerfully as they passed buildings of every size and description. Mother pointed out a house that had probably been built when this was the edge of town. Its corners were neatly dovetailed and the logs had been stained a dark brown, and it nearly blended with the trees. A black and white mongrel dog, much to Carlton's pleasure, sunned himself on the porch while keeping a jaundiced eye on the street. On the next lot stood a long narrow shack of rough wooden shiplap and tarpaper with a canvas upper storey and roof. Mother assumed this to be the temporary home of a large family hastily built before the onset of winter. She realized her mistake when she noticed a rough sign nailed to a post that read: Meals and Bed. It was then that she noticed a trim little log cabin with a red roof directly behind it; the newer rooming house had cut it off from view. Later Mother laughed remembering her indignation, but that day she was sad and disillusioned by the inadequacy of the place.

The street improved as they reached higher ground. Still, it was taking them considerable time to reach the other end. The sun directly overhead soon had them shedding their outer garments. Carlton sat on Dad's knee and looked beautiful as the sun shone on his fair hair. He was attracting the attention of some of the many people who were strolling on the plank sidewalk, with nothing more than a desire to mingle after being cooped up during the recent storm.

A man talking in a group noticed their outfit and came forward. He said that his friend, a freighter whom they had met the night before, asked him to keep an eye out for them in case they needed assistance. The rest of the group were looking Babe and Girlie over with an appreciative eye. Dad, trying to hide his pride in his team, said they were a bit slow but that during the storm they more than made up for it.

Delicious smells drifting towards them from a bakery made my parents realize they were hungry. They had not tasted fresh pastry since leaving Mirror Landing. Dad jumped down and soon emerged from the shop with a huge bag, saying sheepishly that he nearly bought the place out. Munching happily, they continued down the street. They were now passing business places and residences, hardware and general stores, as well as real estate offices, a lumber yard, and several livery stables. So many buildings became a blur, and Mother almost forgot to watch for their hotel. Dad finally spotted it and pointed it out to her.

Sam had learned by moccasin telegraph that my parents and Carlton spent the night at Shaw's Point. He asked Annie, the woman left in charge of the hotel to give the place a quick going-over, then seated by the front window with Brownie at his feet, settled down to read and watch for them. When he caught sight of their rig he tore out to meet them, but Brownie beat him by several lengths. She leapt on them, whining with joy and licking their faces until Sam dragged her off. He said she had nearly gone through the window when she recognized them.

When my parents first saw the hotel they could only stare in dismay. It was hard to believe they had paid so much, and travelled so far, for this shabby square building. It was a far cry from the photograph the Myers had shown them of a new and freshly painted building, its grounds neat and trim. Taking a more realistic view, Dad pointed out that the hotel was solidly built, had fourteen rooms, and was set back from the street. When Sam showed them a tree-shaded area beside the hotel that could be fenced for a playground, Mother brightened. She immediately imagined her children safe, playing with a new sandbox and swing.

Inside, they discovered the usual small lobby, a good-sized dining room with ten tables, a sideboard, and a small parlour at the back for the family. Although there was an air of neglect about the place, Mother, determined to be optimistic, was sure that paint and elbow grease could make it presentable. That was before she saw the kitchen. It was a large well-lit room with plenty of cupboards, but she could not help noticing the filthy congoleum covering the floor. Its pattern was blurred by a film of grease and grime that showed signs of hasty cleaning – the sad-looking mop was still propped in the corner. The afternoon sun shone weakly through windows that had not been washed in months. The walls, darkened by months of smoke and grime, seemed to close in on her. Sam saw her look of dismay and tried to steer her towards the door, hoping to postpone her first encounter with the "capable woman" the Myers had left in charge.

He was too late. With an angry gleam in her eyes, Mother headed toward the sink where Annie Mosquito was industri-ously scrubbing the pots and pans. Annie looked up through long black, stringy hair. A wrinkled calico dress accented her thin, drooping body. As Sam introduced them Annie ducked her head and smiled with her lips while her large black eyes remained fixed on Mother in tragic appeal. Mother felt her anger melt and turn to pity, although she was not sure if what she was feeling was for Annie, or for herself.

With Carlton perched on his shoulder, Sam quickly led the way up the stairs. Brownie was determined not to be left behind again and dived between Sam's legs, nearly upsetting him.

Letting go of Carlton's legs, Sam was able to regain his balance by grabbing hold of the banister. My parents expected tears, but instead Carlton thought it was a new game, and crowed with delight as he clung to Sam's neck. The tension broken, Mother and Dad laughed uproariously as they tried to tell Sam how comical he had looked. Sam found himself sitting on the stairs joining in the hilarity. They regained their composure when Mother pointed to Brownie sitting a few steps above, regarding them with a worried look that seemed to imply that she was the only sane one in the group.

The bedroom – Sam jokingly referred to it as the bridal suite – pleased Mother. Located in a back corner of the building, it was a good size with windows on either side letting in plenty of light. A door opened into a smaller room that was ideal for a nursery. Noticing the crib they had asked Sam to locate, my parents told him how pleased they were. His smile was a bit rueful as he remembered the ribbing he had taken when he inquired around town for it.

Before leaving to unload their sleigh, Sam said he had reserved a table at Ma Nagle's cafe to celebrate their arrival. Ma served the best food in the district. Happy with the turn of events, Mother tucked Carlton into his crib for a nap, then crawled into their nice clean bed for a rest – happy with the thought that it would still be there for her tomorrow.

When they entered the cafe they found it filled to capacity and Sam, who seemed to know everyone, was kept busy introducing them. A short, energetic woman greeted them. This was Mathilde Nagle, or Ma, as everyone called her. Sam said that she was an exceptional woman and like her husband, Al, generous to a fault. Though she had been educated in England and had at one time been a lady-in-waiting in one of the royal households, she was born in Sweden. My parents were intrigued as they watched her treat each customer with the same good humour, regardless of his or her social standing – from garbage collector to bank manager. Her husband had recently bought the Western Hotel. Ma, however, preferred to run this place.

Sam was a favourite customer. His devil-may-care attitude

appealed to Ma's sense of humour. He had been a bit devious, though, mentioning Mother's ancestry to Ma and telling her that Mother appreciated European cuisine. Not knowing this, Mother said that she had not had such a meal since leaving her Aunt Em's. Her aunt, she explained, was Belgian and Dutch.

A bit embarrassed by this sincere compliment, Ma turned to Sam and jokingly accused him of neglecting her, saying that perhaps he preferred Annie Mosquito's cooking. She then told my parent's that Annie was married to a "no-good," who beat her when he got drunk. Annie, however, was known to "hit the ginger" herself. This made Dad more angry than ever with the Myers.

When Ma drifted off to talk to other customers, Sam explained that the Myers had been running the hotel as a rooming house. At present they had eight boarders who would like to stay. My parents decided to continue with these arrangements since my grandmother would not be arriving until May. Grandmother had been apprehensive at first when asked to travel alone into the wilds of northern Canada, but was now looking forward to the trip – at the age of forty-four she had not had many adventures, and the last part by water sounded exciting to her.

As they lingered over coffee, Sam told them about a dubious character who almost got the better of him in a horse trade. He admitted that he had nearly paid cash for the team – they were a well-matched pair and seemed in good condition. Flashing Mother a mischievous grin, he said that a strong hunch made him decide to give them a trial run to his friend's farm. This man had been a freighter and was a good judge of horseflesh. Before he was halfway there, one of the team began showing signs of fatigue, although he had not pushed them. A team good enough to meet demands of freighting was hard to find, Sam's friend told him. He said that this team had been driven hard in extremely cold weather, causing lung damage to one of the horses. Considering himself lucky to have gotten out of that deal, Sam found a good team elsewhere and made a satisfactory swap.

Mother's gaze drifted across the cafe. Her interest was in the silhouette of a young woman across the room. Mother was sure they were in the same condition. Sam noticed the couple as well, and called them over to meet my parents. They were Elsie and Joe Snowball. The two young women nodded politely, while their eyes betrayed pleasure in knowing that the age-old bond of motherhood would draw them together.

The Snowballs were off to the last of a week's dancing hosted by the Hudson's Bay fur traders. Mother refused their invitation at first, saying they were not dressed for dancing. When Elsie insisted, saying dress was optional, she agreed. Sam drove the ladies, while Dad accompanied Joe who had an errand to run.

As Sam helped Mother and Elsie from the sleigh, the plaintive cry of a violin above the chording of a piano and the steady thump of the drum, quickened the heartbeats of the three young people.

"This last dance is the most important social event of the season, and nearly everyone in town will be here," Elsie Snowball whispered excitedly to Mother, "and it's free. The fur traders are hosting it."

Entering the hall, the contrast between the cool outdoor freshness and the blast of hot air, rank with the odour of perspiring, unwashed bodies, almost made them turn back. Sam found it difficult to force his way through a group of men standing four deep inside the door. But when they saw the women, they politely stepped back, letting them through to the dance floor. The stag line extended half-way around the hall. The women and Sam laughed as they dodged the dancers and, gaining the safety of a corner, looked back. A few of the men were all spruced up and anxious to dance. Mother thought that the majority, dressed in heavy mackinaw shirts and trousers, were either freighters or farmers in town for the day and, like themselves, had come to watch. Sam did not agree, saying the reason the men were not dancing was because there were not enough women. As if to prove his point, one of the spectators suddenly sprinted across the floor and claimed an unattached woman.

Mother was surprised to see that many of the women were dressed in formal gowns of the latest fashion, while the townsmen had settled for business or lounge suits. Mixed in were the out-of-towners. The couple that had just danced by was a good example. The man, dressed in rough work clothes, was enjoying himself as he kept perfect time to the music. His partner, a pretty townswoman, was also having a good time. Mother glanced at Elsie who reminded her that their dress was acceptable.

The only empty bench was below the stage above which the music makers sat. Mother watched them with great interest. The piano player, partly hidden by his instrument, gazed at the crowd while he pounded out the tunes. The drummer never looked up and seemed to be mesmerized by his steady beat. The most interesting was the leader of the group, the fiddler. With tapping foot and bow flying, he and his fiddle became one, sending forth a rollicking tune that made the place come alive. It was too much for Sam and Mother. Carried away by the music, Sam led her onto the dance floor, leaving Elsie to watch for the Dad and Joe.

Meanwhile, Dad was waiting patiently for Joe to finish his errand. After tethering the team, Joe had left with a package saying it was a part for a seeder he had promised to deliver. He was taking a long time and Dad was about to go in without him, when Joe returned with friends, Dan Hayden and Tom Riley. They had been discussing Dad's team. They told Dad that their neighbour was William McCue, the man who had recently bought the Percheron stallion that Dad had earlier heard about. Dad asked if they knew of a stable that rented space by the month and Dan told him that he knew of a place that might be suitable. Then, remembering the waiting wives, Dad arranged to meet them in the morning.

Finding the women and Sam in a crowded hall might have been difficult if a friend of Joe's had not pointed out Elsie. Dad looked for Sam and Mother and was astonished when he spotted Sam's long legs executing the intricate steps of a Scottish reel, and Mother, hardly showing the condition she was usually so self-conscious of, dancing with gay abandon. Dad heaved a sigh when the dance finally ended thinking he would have her all to himself, but was a bit put out when Joe swept her away for the next dance. As he watched, he felt that he was seeing his wife in a new light. He wished now he had learned to dance. But in Africa he had always shied away from the social side of life, preferring his long trips into the veldt and bush land.

The waltzes ended and the women, flushed and happy, were ready to leave. Sam, however, decided to stay till the end. Elsie was anxious for a chat so she climbed into the back seat of the sleigh with Mother. It did not take them long to discover that both babies would be born in July. This was to be the Snowball's first child, for they had been married less than a year. Joe told Mother he had been in Grouard a year before he returned to eastern Canada for Elsie. They had been married the past June. Their trip by rail and steamboat to Grouard was their honeymoon. Mother laughed, saying she too had come from the east – Buffalo, New York.

As they approached the hotel, Dad said it looked almost respectable in the soft moonlight. Mother agreed, adding that what pleased her most was how wonderful it was going to be sleeping in a comfortable bed after weeks of not knowing whether they would be sleeping on a hard bunk, or on spruce boughs in some drafty corner. Knowing this to be a concession, Dad picked her up and carried her to their room. It was partly to show his happiness, but he was also concerned for her health. He was afraid she had overdone it with the dancing.

Her pale face showed how close she was to exhaustion. Still, he thought the dance had been the right approach, showing her that even in a remote boom town such as this, people found enjoyment as in any other civilized place. He advised her to sleep in in the morning – he intended to ask Sam to look after Carlton while he met his friends at the stable.

Dad was soon asleep, but Mother found it hard to unwind. She lay thinking of her dilemma. Annie would have to stay until after her delivery and she regained her strength. By then there would be two babies to look after, and food to cook and serve.

Her mother was arriving in the spring, but she had doubts about how helpful she would be. It seemed her troubles had multiplied. Looking on the brighter side – Dad, she knew, was determined to make a success of the hotel. He had already had stern words with Annie, telling her that she must arrive on time, and start cleaning up the place. Mother knew that he was not fooled by Annie's demure attitude. Reassured, she fell asleep.

CHAPTER ELEVEN

Hotels and Homesteads

The grey dawn had begun to lighten in the deep indigo sky when Dad entered the kitchen carrying his sharp axe and an old Edmonton *Bulletin*. He was prepared to light the handsome six-burner Stewart range that caught his eye the day before. When he discovered the split white pine in the woodbox, he knew he was in luck. This particular wood gave off a fast, intense heat.

He filled the big coffee pot with water and dumped in a generous amount of coffee, then, noticing its blackened sides, he removed the stove lid and placed the pot directly over the flames. Stepping into the shed for some greener wood, he returned to find the coffee had boiled over. A bit dismayed at the mess, he looked in vain for a dishcloth in order to clean it up. He shrugged it off – a few coffee grounds would not disturb Annie. At any rate he had made plenty of coffee, hoping his new friends would return with him.

Looking at his watch, he realized he would have to hurry if he was going to feed and water his team before meeting Dan and Tom. He knew that he was on the spot with Mother – he had promised to look after Carlton this morning to let her sleep in. He had hoped Sam would help him out but had found him in a deep sleep and been unable to rouse him.

Shrugging on his coat and grabbing his mitts, he headed for the door and nearly ran over Annie. Dad hardly recognized her, she looked so clean and neat – black hair shining and a fresh dress showing under her old moosehide jacket. On impulse, he asked her to look after Carlton as he did not want Ollie disturbed for a while, then remembered to tell Annie to warm the buns and pastries as he would likely be bringing a couple of friends back shortly.

Last night's heavy frost had stiffened the puddles into ice that crackled under Dad's heavy boots. He was relieved that the warm spell had not lasted. He needed time to locate a heavy wagon he could convert into a dray in order to haul freight around town and the nearby district. This would put his heavy team to good use and earn the family a few extra dollars. Freighting work should be plentiful once the boats started running.

Mother had no intention of sleeping in and missing Dad's new friends. The dance had given Mother a chance to observe a few of the different personalities that made up the town, and she was interested in meeting some of them. Hearing him leave, she tried to get up but drifted off again, still in a blissful state of semiconsciousness. Dad was right. She was very weary. It was an hour before she was fully awake. Opening the door, she listened to Carlton's prattle and expected to hear Sam answer him. Instead, Annie's soft voice drifted up to her. Sam, she rightly surmised was still asleep.

Dad waited at the stables for over an hour and was about to leave when Dan showed up alone. He apologized, saying, "I've been searching everywhere for Tom, and believe he must be off on a bender. I suspected this when someone at the dance slipped him a bottle, but hoped he'd sleep it off. Instead, he had gone out after another one. I'd like to know where he got the liquor. We were together most of the evening."

An understanding look came into Dan's eyes when Dad mentioned the parcel Snowball gave Tom last evening. "I believe, he said it was a part for his seeder, if I recall rightly," Dad said.

Dan laughed. "Tom doesn't own a seeder, but he gets a powerful thirst whenever he comes to town."

With a puzzled look on his face, Dad said, "I thought Snowball was an implement dealer."

Dan nodded. "He is, but it's also rumoured that he deals in bootleg liquor, and in Grouard it's never wise to ask questions or look for labels."

"What Snowball does is his business, and makes no difference to me, but I hope Ollie doesn't find out. She might not look at it that way, and she's taken quite a shine to Snowball's wife."

This led to a discussion about the notorious bootlegger, Baldy Red, a character widely known throughout the Peace River Country.

"Baldy," Dan said, "liked to boast that the secret of his bootlegging success was that he never used the same tactics twice. The police kept a sharp eye on him and were especially suspicious of the freight he carried. He was heading north with a load of contraband goods one summer day when he was overtaken by a well-respected clergyman from Grande Prairie who seemed to be having trouble with his team of highly-spirited young horses. Baldy, who was also heading for Grande Prairie, noticed the reverend gentleman's uneasiness when his skittish team reared up and shied while passing him. 'That's a frisky team, Reverend,' said Baldy, and the minister agreed. 'I've an idea. Why don't you drive my quiet team the rest of the way, and I'll drive yours.' The minister agreed and innocently drove Baldy's booze past the Mounties and into Grande Prairie to Baldy's barn, where the whisky was later unloaded by his hired man. In the meantime, Baldy Red drove the minister's team.

"Baldy was a likable rascal, even if he did become attached to stray cows and horses and then considered them his property. Tales of his scrapes became legendary, and though he usually got off scot free, on one occasion he was not so lucky and was sent down the trail to Peace River to appear before the magistrate on a charge of cattle theft. While able to overlook his own short-comings, he loathed petty thievery. The Mountie on this trip was also bringing in a man charged with stealing a watch. Feeling he was above this, Baldy treated the alleged watch thief with contempt, refusing to have anything to do with him. But every now and then, Baldy harassed him by asking him the time of day.

"Over and over, as they travelled the long trail from Grande Prairie to Waterhole, Griffin Creek, and down the hills to Shaftsbury Settlement, the Mountie and the petty thief heard Baldy's strident voice, wanting to know the time. Finally, goaded beyond endurance, the watch thief could take no more. When Baldy the cow-napper again asked, 'What time is it?' the thief pulled himself up and replied, 'Milking time, you son of a - - - - -.' "

The two men chuckled over the scrapes of Baldy Red. Babe and Girlie stood patiently, tails swishing and heads nodding, as if in agreement. Their dappled gray coats gleamed in the sun. Dan admired their matched beauty. Thinking about their need for pasture, he remembered a homestead on the outskirts of town that had been abandoned. "The owner was hoping to make a deal with any interested party through the Land Titles Office for the land and improvements – the usual small cabin and barn. The land is heavily timbered, with only a few acres cleared. It has the advantage though, of being in the general area of your hotel," he added.

"It sounds to me like a good deal," Dad replied, "and as I've said, I'm desperate for a place for my team."

The tantalizing aroma of coffee mingling with bacon and pancakes made Mother realize she was starving. On entering the dining room she was relieved that there was no sign of the boarders – only Carlton sat there, stuffing down the last of his pancakes and Annie hovered nearby. She had made him a high chair by placing several cushions under him and tied him to the chair with a tea towel around his middle. She had also tied one around his neck as a bib, but his hands, face, even his hair was covered with thick, sticky syrup and bits of food. The table was a mess although Brownie had cleaned up the floor beneath.

When he spotted Mother, Carlton immediately demanded to be taken up. She was just debating whether or not to ruin her last clean dress when Sam appeared in the doorway and, sizing up the situation, scooped Carlton from his chair and headed with him toward the kitchen. Glancing over his shoulder, Sam grinned at Mother and nodded toward the window where Dad and Dan could be seen coming up the walk. Hearing Carlton's shrill laughter from the kitchen, Mother smiled as she hurried to the front door, imagining Sam amusing the baby with one of his silly antics. This young friend, who was always helping her out, might have been one of the twin brothers she lost so many years ago. He had the same blond hair, same blue eyes, and was even the same age.

There was a smile in Dad's voice as he introduced Mother to his new friend. He told her they had shared similar experiences. Born in Gagetown, New Brunswick, Dan Hayden had also answered the call to arms during the Boer War and served with the Canadian Dragoons. Shortly after his return to Canada, he headed west, arriving in Edmonton in 1904. He freighted around the Westaskwin area for a couple of years before coming north to Grouard. During the summer, he said, his trips often took him to Peace River Crossing, Waterhole, Bear Lake, and points west. He was fortunate, he explained, because Fletcher Breden, the area's first representative in the newly-formed Government of Alberta, made road building a major responsibility. In 1906 he had received two thousand dollars for improving the old cart trail, widening it, building bridges, culverts, and long stretches of corduroy over the worst stretches. "Still," Dan said, "my friends and I spent many hours up to our knees in mud while digging each other out. But in spite of hardships winter and summer, I wouldn't have missed sharing the good times I had on the trail with my buddies. However, farming my own land has been the greatest experience of all." Referring to his single status, he said while looking at Mother with a twinkle in his eyes, "If I'd had the good fortune of meeting you first, it might have been a different story," winning her over completely.

After they had demolished stacks of Annie's pancakes, Dad's coffee, and the last of the bacon, Mother asked Dan what he knew about the handsome fiddler who had entertained them at the dance. He said that his name was William Gardner. He was known as Billy and was the best fiddler in the district. Billy was born in Fort Chipewyan and like other young men of the area started out tracking sturgeon-head boats. He often laughed when he recalled some of his experiences on the job. However, it was not the back-breaking toil that stuck in his mind, it was the terrible food they had had to endure – all for a wage of fifteen dollars a trip from Athabasca Landing to the site of the present Grouard. Pay was thirty skins at fifty cents each in currency. Billy returned to Fort Chipewyan as an employee of the Company, where his diligence gained him prominence, and where he learned the art of fiddling. Both his fiddles had been made at the fort. Billy was very popular and known throughout the district as a great friend and a natural charmer.

"However," Dan said, "there is another side to him that most people don't know. He has worked for years to ease the suffering of the Natives in the area."

Dad interrupted, saying, "I've been told that the Klondikers were responsible for the plight of the Indians around here."

Dan agreed. "Many half-breeds and Indians starved to death when gold-seekers were forced to trap the forests of Lesser Slave Lake and along the Peace River. They used poison bait for wolves that killed off hundreds of Indian dogs, leaving the Indians stranded. Their dogs were their only means of transportation."

At first, the Natives welcomed white traders to their tribal lands, especially when they were offered what seemed to them priceless treasures – traps, sharp knives, axes, cooking pots, and beads, in exchange for furs which were relatively easy for them to obtain.

Before signing Treaty 8 in 1899, all the land in the Peace River Country belonged to these people. As well as trespassing, the Klondikers heaped abuse on the Indians by deliberately setting off their bear traps after one of the white man's horses had accidently stepped in one. They also pilfered food the Indians had cached in trees for their return trips from the hunting grounds.

The old timers tell of a famine among the Indians at Peace River Crossing well over a hundred years ago. They were rescued by the Hudson's Bay Company who sent oxen-drawn Red River carts to bring them to a site, now Grouard, on Lesser Slave Lake. More than a hundred survivors lived off the bounty of the lake. The lake is deep and clean with white sandy beaches. Old Lamoose says that before the white man came, it was filled with white fish, pickerel, jackfish, and trout. The Indians built high scaffolds and dried the fish on them for winter food for themselves and their dogs. Old timers remember that over a hundred thousand fish at a time could be seen drying on the scaffolds.

Some Métis – the offspring of Native women and white fur traders – finding they belonged neither to the Indians' or the white men's world, headed north and settled along Lesser Slave Lake. Among them were followers of Louis Riel who made the long trek across the plains from Fort Gary after the Rebellion, as well as many Iroquois boatmen looking for a new life after the fur trade in more southerly areas dwindled. Many of the descendants of these people still hunt and trap in the foothills of the Smoky River's headwaters. A number of Father Lacombe's flock also joined the migration and, by 1913, the year my parents arrived in Grouard, this race of mixed bloods, called Métis by the French and half breeds by the English, made up the majority of the area's population. These people had Billy Gardner's sympathy, for he knew their story. Billy was in great demand as a fiddler, especially during the winter months when hardly a night went by without a dance or party in the home of one of his Métis friends.

"Tall and well-built," Dan went on, "this generation seems to combine the best of both races and, although industrious and well-liked, they are a devil-may-care lot and, if the evening's entertainment is held at Dakota Jim's, or Doctor Tullock's place, it is bound to be lively, with plenty of 'Ginger' or 'Moose Milk.' Prohibition does not bother these people – they consider that half the fun is helping smugglers bring in the contraband whiskey."

121

Smuggling booze was no easy task with Sergeant Anderson of the Mounted Police in charge. However, Dan considered that the police and the smugglers were well matched when it came to outwitting each other. He laughed as he said, "I remember the day two scows were seen pulling into Shaw's Point. A police boat headed over to investigate. One scow docked and its crew began to unload with much haste. The police boat rushed alongside and, with great anticipation, carefully inspected its contents. Meanwhile, the other scow proceeded to Grouard and, while the attention of the police was occupied with the liquorless scow, its crew unloaded their cases of Moose Milk and cached them away in Kan-ne-kan's teepee. To be sure, there was a party in one of the homes along Bouillon Street before the night was over. With so little to do during the long cold winters, they danced the night away."

My parents were to learn that Fort Chipewyan was not the only place in the north that could produce a fiddle. Dave McKinnon told this story about a *moochigan* held in a country store that he and his brother had nearly completed building. Everyone was having a good time, although the men had to wait their turn for a dance as there were only ten women to thirty men, mostly bachelor homesteaders. The music was provided by Bill Cross, a young man who had recently filed on a quarter-section near High Prairie. Perhaps like Mother, he too had become mesmerized by Billy's fiddling, and that is why he decided to make a fiddle for himself. Using birch for the back and spruce for the front, he carved the tailpiece and pegs from the shinbone of a cayuse, pulled hair from a horse's tail for the bow, then learned to play his instrument. Although his friends and neighbours were intrigued by his ingenious use of materials, it was not until twenty years later when visiting Bill in Vancouver, that Dave was to discover that his friend's first attempt at fiddle-making was not just a lucky fluke. Cross, who was working as a longshoreman at the time, still made fiddles as a sideline. As proof of his proficiency, he had just sold one to the orchestra leader of the Pantages Theatre.

Bill Cross fit right in with the settlers. The story of brave

Mrs. Sophia Smith and her family is incomplete without him. Mrs. Smith, her husband, their thirty-one-year-old son Henry, and four of their daughters, ranging in age from seven to fifteen, arrived in Red Deer in 1912 to look for a homestead between there and Rocky Mountain House. But within ten months Mr. Smith was dead. After the funeral, this fifty-two-year-old woman – who had borne seventeen children – decided to carry out their plans to locate a homestead. A newspaper account of the fabled Peace River Country helped her decide to head there while she still had the money to do so. She and her children purchased a team and wagon, two cows to freshen, some chickens, a mower, hayrack, plow, disk and harrows, and loaded them along with their household goods onto a freight train headed for Athabasca Landing. The family then boarded a mixed train from Edmonton. At times the train moved so slowly that the passengers could run along beside it. At that, they made the ninety-mile trip from Edmonton to the Landing in just one day.

On June 7, 1913, they arrived at Athabasca Landing, where they sent most of their possessions on to Grouard by boat. Henry then made arrangements for them to join a wagon train for the remaining two hundred miles of their trip to Grouard. Travelling with them were Mr. and Mrs. Elmer Brodie, a honeymooning couple who would be their neighbours for many years. Another young couple with a six-month-old baby, wanting to make better time, left earlier. When the wagon train caught up with them, they discovered the baby had died. The young mother, in a state of shock and grief, had been unable to eat for days. Mrs. Smith had brought along a bottle of brandy for medicinal purposes and hoped it might help the young woman, but the men had already discovered it and drunk it all.

One of the cows calved, making it necessary for Henry to take the newborn calf by horseback several miles distance, back to Athabasca Landing. Meanwhile, the others went on and the trip was a rough one. The girls walked the entire distance herding the cows and calves, wearing out three pairs of shoes each. At night, after pitching their tents, the family scooped holes in the ground to fit their bodies, placed mosquito netting over their blankets, and it was here the tired pioneers slept. Many times they awoke to discover the holes had filled with water from a muskeg bog near them. In the morning, armed with willow branches to keep off the insects, they carried on. The livestock suffered most, as the gnats and "no-see-ums" attacked their ears, at times sending them into a frenzy. However, the milk from the cows and fresh eggs from their chickens added to their fare, and even the youngest daughter learned to bake very good bannock.

Following the Athabasca River, they came to a portage and watched as passengers from a boat disembarked. Everything, including passengers had to be unloaded and packed either on the backs of horses or onto special packboards carried by men by means of straps that were braced around their foreheads. At the portage they saw a four-horse team get stuck in the mud trying to pull an empty wagon downhill. The Smiths winched their way from Mirror Landing to Soto Landing on Lesser Slave River with block and tackle, thankful it was only a few miles. At Soto they watched the boat dock again and its passengers reboarded to resume the trip by water.

Most of the wagons in the train crossed the Moose River, travelling along the south side of Lesser Slave Lake, along the route of the present Number 2 Highway. However, the Smiths chose the rocky road along the north shore after learning the other road passed through muskeg. The north shore road was so bad, no one attempted to ride in the wagon or even drive the horses. They just proceeded slowly, picking their way through the rocks.

Henry, who by then had rejoined the party, was able to get them across the Martin River in June flood by first tying a long rope to a tree, swimming a horse across to the opposite side of the river, and tying the other end of the rope to a tree. Using the rope as a guideline, they drove the stock into the river to swim them across. Mrs. Smith and the girls rode the wagon attached to a cable which was pulled across the water by the horses. It took them an entire day to get everything to the other shore.

The enjoyable part of the adventure was that wild strawberries and other berries were beginning to ripen in plentiful supply. Mrs. Smith claimed that the bears liked the berries too and it was a toss up who left the patches first, the bears or the girls.

Arriving in Grouard on June 28, the Smith camp was set up amidst a small army of tents on Hudson's Bay Hill. The town was bursting its seams. Not only were new settlers coming over the trail and on every boat, people had been coming from as far as Grande Prairie, Dunvegan, Waterhole, Peace River Crossing, and High Prairie for the annual First of July sports day, held at Buffalo Bay. The Smiths clothes were in a sad state after nearly a month on the trail, but Ma Burchell, a kind woman who ran a store in Buffalo Bay, outfitted the girls for the sports day, free of charge.

It was the big event of the year with horse racing, bronco busting, foot-racing, a tug-a-war, and good times for young and old. Added to all this were colourful Indian tee pees. Natives had been holding their pow-wow in honour of the Great White Mother on this site since 1814, the year of Waterloo. Tom-toms and the cry of the fiddle were heard all night as the *moochigan* went on night after night.

During the celebration, Henry Smith met Billy Cross and the common bond of playing the fiddle cemented their friendship. When Billy found out that the Smiths' plans were still only at the hopeful stage, he suggested property near his own homestead and assisted them to file on it. The Smiths agreed.

After a wonderful week in Grouard, the Smiths packed their gear and set off again, crossing the long bridge that was still partially covered with water from the June flood. They were full of anticipation at the prospect of seeing their new land. They spent their first night camping on the homestead of Pete Neilson and his wife, where they were treated to their first meal served at a table since leaving Edmonton.

They reached East Prairie River next day and found it in flood so they set up camp on its banks, where they were visited by some of the people who would be their neighbours, including Dan Hayden, O. D. Hill, and Sid Savill. The next morning these men helped the family across the river, and the Smiths pressed on to their next camp at West Prairie River where Billy Cross had arranged to meet them. Taking charge, he helped them across the river, then recruited some of his bachelor friends to cut a trail to the two quarter sections he had helped the Smiths file on. It was next to his own land. He and his friends were able to assist the Smiths to erect a sod-roofed cabin on their place. Billy Cross exemplified the true pioneer spirit of mutual sharing and endurance. Mrs. Smith, who lived to the age of ninety-seven, also proved to be a wonderful example of the district's early pioneers.

• • •

After a month of painting and cleaning, my parents' hotel was greatly improved. Most of the painting had been done by two of the boarders who were happy to have something to do while waiting for spring break-up. Mother and Annie had put in long days organizing the kitchen and getting the rest of the place in order. Mother improved the menu with the help of a dog-eared cook book that contained her favourite recipes – mostly Aunt Em's. She had thought there were enough demands on her without this extra work, but looking back, she realized that there had been a good side to it. She could be rigid and judgmental and after their first meeting had formed negative feelings toward Annie. Letting go of a grudge had not been easy. Both she and Annie had come a long way since then. For Annie, the turning point had been when Dad asked her if she would care for Carlton that first morning.

Meanwhile, Dad took Dan's advice and made a deal with the Land Titles Office to take over the abandoned homestead. Through this transaction he met William Stewart, manager of the Royal Bank. A few days later his wife, Susan, came to call. Though Susan smiled pleasantly, Mother got the impression that nothing escaped her piercing blue eyes.

Mother remembered seeing Susan Stewart and her husband

at Ma Nagle's restaurant and thinking that they were a striking couple. Mrs. Stewart had also noticed my parents. "I asked Mr. Stewart then who the newcomers were," she said, surprising my mother with her Scottish accent. "Remembering my interest, he mentioned yesterday that he had again met your husband – the new owner of this hotel – and I decided to call and welcome you to Grouard."

Mother, used to the impersonal attitudes in a city, felt warmed by this small-town friendliness shown to a stranger. Before she was able to thank her, Carlton cried to be taken up after his nap. She reached for the bell to call Annie then started for the door herself, saying that after being with her small son constantly during the long trip, he was sometimes upset if he awakened and found himself alone.

"What a bonny child!" Mrs. Stewart exclaimed when Mother returned with Carlton. As she gazed at him, a look of sadness seemed to darken her blue eyes and for a moment she seemed a softer, more vulnerable person. Many years later, my mother remembered this incident when she learned that Mrs. Stewart had lost her only child in infancy.

Just as Mother was about to call for Annie, she appeared in the doorway. Seeing a visitor, she hesitated and with an embarrassed look tried to straighten her untidy dress. Then with a defiant shrug, she darted across the room, picked up Carlton, and was out the door before Mother could ask her to bring them tea. Mother looked at Mrs. Stewart, not knowing whether to apologize or to ignore Annie's strange behaviour. She had looked so comical though, that as their eyes met they burst into laughter. Mother, previously a bit intimidated by Susan Stewart, was happy to find that they had a similar sense of humour. Perhaps it was her Gaelic upbringing that would not allow Mrs. Stewart to be carried away too far. With eyes still laughing, she managed to say in a rather severe tone, the Scottish accent even more pronounced, "I've learned from experience that one must always keep a firm upper hand." Then, in a friendly way, she congratulated Mother on the improvements already made.

Mother admitted that the place had been in a bad state when they first arrived. "However, we all pitched in, and although there is still a lot to do, we've made a start. As for Annie," she said with a smile, "I could no more train her than harness the wind. It is Carlton who has won her over. Being a mother herself, she realized that I needed help with such an active child, and just took over." Mother remembered the day Annie had turned up distraught and badly beaten by her drunken husband. It was easier to overlook a few undesirable traits after that. "Besides," she went on to say, "with two small children to support, they barely exist on her salary. Her husband traps in the winter, but drinks and gambles away most of it."

Mrs. Stewart said she had heard that many of the Natives were living in great poverty, and that she would organize a drive to help these needy families. Before they could discuss it further, Annie arrived with their tea.

Mrs. Stewart then explained that her real reason for calling so soon was to invite Mother to a tea to meet the local women. Mother hesitated, saying that although she knew it would be very enjoyable, she would have to refuse as it would be some time before she could repay the hospitality. "I understand," Mrs. Stewart answered, "and so will the women you will meet. Most of them have helped their husbands get started in business. But we wives must support one another in an outpost such as this." When Mother still hesitated, Mrs. Stewart tried another approach: "The ladies will be interested in meeting you and hearing how you survived that terrible storm." Mother relented and accepted the invitation.

The tea was a huge success, as were all of Mrs. Stewart's undertakings. It was a large affair, giving the women an opportunity to visit with friends from town, as well as out of town, and Mother a chance to meet them all. Mrs. Pottage, wife of Frank Pottage, a lawyer and businessman, was given the honour of pouring tea. The Pottages, Mother learned, owned the finest house in town. She also met Mrs. Field, whose husband was in charge of the RNWMP detachment. Mother took the opportunity to tell her how impressed they had been with the neat barracks and the young officers who had greeted her and Dad when they had first arrived. Mrs. Field answered that there was very little crime to keep them busy during the winter – except the local bootleggers.

Mother recalled seeing many of the ladies at the Hudson's Bay dance. She remembered one in particular who was considerably younger than the rest. Slim and strikingly dark, she was introduced as Mrs. Harvey, wife of the Hudson's Bay Company factor. She took Mother's hand in a friendly manner and with a dazzling smile asked to be called Sissie. Another interesting woman was Mrs. McDermott, wife of the Indian agent, who was said to be an Indian princess, and whose family was a credit to the town.

In the years to come Susan Stewart was to be greatly respected as the social leader of Grouard and, later, Peace River. Her rigid sense of propriety usually had a good influence on both young and old. There were few, however, who did not take kindly to her attempts at straightening them out. I was too well brought up to let it show, but I must admit I too felt a bit hostile when Mrs. Stewart took me, at age twenty-one, to task for displaying too much exuberance when I made my first and only hole-in-one while playing golf with Mr. Stewart and my husband, Ged. However, I apologized when I recalled past kindnesses to me. I remembered once when I was ten and a half, Mrs. Stewart decided to produce a "Good Health" play for the children of Peace River, and chose me to take the part of the Sunshine Fairy. It is hard to describe the pleasure that such an event brought to a shy country child like me.

On the night before the play opened, Mrs. Stewart asked Nettie Rumble and me to spend the night at her home, knowing we would have to practice later than usual. Instead of staying in town after school to play with friends, my brothers and I had to trudge the four miles home, often in bitter winter weather. (Cars were put up on blocks until spring in those days.) Later she went to the trouble of informing my mother that I was a well-brought-up little girl; that I insisted on helping with the dishes, while my younger friend Nettie listened to the radio for the first time. The Stewarts were among the few in Peace River to own a radio in 1923. When the dishes were done, Mr. Stewart separated the earphones to let us both listen. It seemed like magic as the announcer's voice and music came over the air. Our family had no radio, but we had music in our home since the early homestead days when my parents had to choose between a gramophone and a cream separator. It was really no choice. We all voted for the gramophone, and Mother kept on skimming off the cream by hand. I can still hear the voice of Harry Lauder, coming through the large horn that topped the old-fashioned wind-up machine.

At Susan Stewart's tea Mother also met Lelia Anderson, a lovely lady who had been a missionary at White Fish Lake. In 1905, she became the bride of St. Sgt. Kristian F. Anderson, who became one of the Peace River Country's most famous police officers. Of Icelandic descent, Sgt. Anderson, known as Andy, had quite a reputation in Grouard as a sailor. He often bucked the gale-whipped lake in his Peterborough canoe, patrolling in pursuit of smugglers on days when no one else dared venture out.

Anderson was a policeman who never gave up until he brought his man to justice. Over six feet in height and two-hundred pounds of hard muscle and brawn, he always managed to overtake his prey, plodding on through howling winds and bitter cold, often without food or sleep. Yet, on more than one occasion, he had grubstaked a criminal out of his own pocket to give the man a fresh start after having served his term.

Anderson played a major role in an infamous murder case in the area. This is the account of the King murder that took place at Sucker Creek, southwest of Grouard, as told by Agnes Cameron.

In September 1904, the Indians reported to the Mounted Police that they had seen two white men travelling together in the early summer, but that afterwards one man walked alone and was now at Grouard. An observant Cree boy added, "The dogs won't follow that other white fellow anymore." Sergeant Anderson went to their last known camp and discovered in the turned-over ashes of the campfire three hard lumps of flesh and a small piece of skull bone. Convinced that murder had been done, he arrested the suspected man and sent him to Fort Saskatchewan for trial.

No one knew the identity of either the dead man or the living. In front of the old camp-fire was a little slough or lake, and this seemed to Anderson a promising place to look for evidence. Sergeant Anderson hired Indian women to wade into the ooze, feeling with their toes for any hard substance. In this way were secured a sovereign case and a stickpin of unusual make. The slough was then systematically drained and yielded a shoe with a broken-eyed needle sticking in it. Sifting the ashes of the campfire and examining them with a microscope established a connection between the burnt flesh and the exhibits from the lake. The maker of the stickpin in London, England, was cabled by the Canadian government; the stick pin was traced to its purchaser, a man named Edward Hayward. His brother was found and summoned from London to identify his brother's belongings. A cheque drawn by the dead Hayward in favour of King came to the surface in a British Columbia bank. Link by link by link the chain of evidence grew.

It took eleven months for Sergeant Anderson to get his case in shape. Then he convoyed forty Indian witnesses two hundred and fifty miles from Grouard to Edmonton to tell what they knew about the crime committed in the silent places. The evidence they helped to uncover was placed before the jury and the Indians returned home. A legal technicality cropped up and the trial had to be repeated. Once more the forty Indians travelled from Grouard to repeat the story. The result was that Charles King of Utah was found guilty of the murder of Edward Hayward and paid the death penalty.

Another, this time more amusing, tale of Sergeant Anderson was written by Jean Cameron Kelly, for the local history, 'I Remember' Peace River, Alberta (Peace River: Peace River Women's Institute, 1976).

A number of dogs once roamed the streets [of

Peace River Crossing], apparently homeless, but regarded as individuals in their own right. Among these was Diamond P. Toby, one of the gayest and most gallant-hearted of the Peace River pioneers. He was the result of a misalliance between a pure bred Great Dane mother, owned by somebody over in Grouard, and a legendary sled-dog named Chimo. . . . Chimo was a sort of huge mongrel-coyote-hound-cum-Russian-wolfhound, and some of his progeny were the biggest dogs I have ever seen. . . .

Toby was rumoured to be an interested spectator of an event which reportedly took place when Sergeant Anderson encountered one of the Corporals, a scrappy Irishman named Casson, whom the sergeant suspected of having gotten away with some confiscated boot-leg liquor. The story goes that the Sergeant was returning home and met Casson going to town with what the Sergeant considered a suspicious-looking parcel under his arm, and Toby at his heels. The Sergeant roared, 'What is that?' and the Corporal roared back, 'None of your (censored) business!'

The parcel was a perfectly innocent cake which Mrs. Anderson had baked for the dance that night, and had requested the corporal to deliver. Casson set the cake in the snow when his determination to proceed to the dance met head-on with the Sergeant's determination to take him back to the barracks for insubordination. I never did learn who won, unless it was Toby, who had been sniffing hopefully after the cake all along, and demolished it with gusto during the fracas. [p. 55]

While doing research for this book, I interviewed Sam Simpson. He and his wife lived in the Peace district and he was still sprightly and active, although in his nineties. He told me an amusing story that throws light on Sergeant Anderson's reason for being suspicious:

"Casson had been sent to Grouard to bring back a prisoner who had been caught with a case of contraband booze. The two young men were about the same age and on the trail back, formed a friendship based on their Irish heritage and liking for strong drink. They joked and laughed as they jolted over the corduroy road that the prisoner called the Rocky Road to Dublin.

"As they approached the last campground before crossing the Crooked Creek Bridge, Corporal Casson succumbed to the temptation to break into the case of whiskey he was bringing back as evidence – egged on by the prisoner's hints as to it's smoothness, and how a belt or two would ease the humiliation of being thrown into jail.

"The next thing they knew, they were being dragged from the ditch where they had passed out, by the furious Sergeant Anderson. He had come looking for them after the team made it back to Peace River on its own. Casson, in deep trouble because the rest of the whiskey had disappeared, was soundly whipped by Anderson." (Although I can not be sure of this, my lawyer husband says the case would likely have been dismissed through lack of evidence, and the prisoner set free.)

In 1916, Anderson was made divisional inspector and served the Peace country until his retirement.

ABOVE:
Mother at sixteen.

RIGHT:
Me, 4, and Wilbur, 2, on our homestead.

ABOVE:
Clockwise from top right: Me,
Warren, Wilbur, and Carlton.

RIGHT:
My mother made my lovely bonnet
from twisted crepe paper.

135

ABOVE:
Clockwise from top: Dad, me, Wilbur Junior, Mother, Marjorie, Warren, and Carlton. 1920.

LEFT:
Aunt Eva, on her visit to Peace River in 1921.

Dad, standing in his oatfield.

Dad with his prize-winning cabbages grown on the Shaftsbury Farm.

CHAPTER TWELVE

Grandmother

It was a happy time, those first ten weeks of my parents' stay in Grouard. The days were sunny, but with freezing nights the lake was slow in breaking up. Transportation from the south was at a standstill and business was slow. This meant my grandmother would not be arriving until around the first of June. Taking advantage of the lull, my parents explored the countryside, often driving out to their homestead where Dad was extending the pasture fences.

Living so close to nature was a new experience for Mother. She was amazed at the lush beauty of the countryside and sudden change of seasons. The trees – poplar, birch, and willow – brazenly bare in winter, were suddenly clothed in every shade of green. Even the drab evergreens were a brighter hue. In the high blue sky, returning wild geese beat the air with strong wings. Their cry never failed to thrill her. She and Dad often stopped the team to watch them pass. They enjoyed driving to a secluded spot on the lakeshore, to watch the ice slowly disappear. Dad taught his small son to throw stones into the water. They laughed, sharing his delight, when he pointed to the circles growing wider and wider and yelled, "Daddy, Mommy, look at the funny water!" Trixie, newly reunited with the family, was ecstatic. The dogs chased each other up and down the beach. Little Trixie did not seem to mind when Brownie's long legs out-distanced him every time.

Sam had brought Trixie to Grouard on his last trip from Edmonton. "Never again," he told my parents. "That little dog thinks he's a Doberman. He stood his ground against an Indian's husky. The big brute lunged at him and would have torn him to pieces if the animal's chain had been a few inches longer." Glaring at Mother, Dad said, "I told you, Ollie; we should have left him with the Henderson's. Now, he could be killed by one of the big brutes that roams the streets." She refused to be intimidated. Her answer was, "And so could I be killed by one of the drunken brutes that roam the streets. Trixie helped me through my homesickness, Wilbur, and I won't abandon him now."

In early June, the Hudson's Bay boat brought Grandmother to Grouard from Calgary, where she had been living. During the intervening time, Mother had had time to become reconciled to the past. Her own motherhood had helped her realize it could not have been easy, years ago, for her mother to give her up to Aunt Em. Mother's thoughts leapt back and she was once again the small child, crying in the night, first for the father to whom she had been so close and then for the mother she had lost. It had frightened her even more when Aunt Em hid her from her father who had tried to steal her. She had come to love her foster parents greatly, particularly Aunt Em, who in her heart would always be her real mother.

As her resentment toward Grandmother faded, Mother came to grips, too, with her feelings toward Edward, her sister's child, whom her mother was bringing with her. She remembered the furore his birth had caused. Grandmother had refused to let Eve give him up and supported her young daughter when the child's father refused to take any responsibility for him. They had taken him to court and won their case, for Edward, then a year old, was the image of his father. It did little good. The young man paid half of the medical expenses and vanished, leaving my grandmother with another responsibility. A short time later, Eve married but was seldom around to care for her son. Now, Grandmother was arriving with the boy.

That June day, a deep-throated blast from a mile out warned the bridge attendant of the approaching steamboat, giving him time to open the drawbridge. The captain pulled the whistle twice more, causing great excitement on shore. Everyone dropped what they were doing and rushed down to watch the first boat of the season, the *Grahame*, slowly slip into her berth at the end of Main Street Bridge. This was the first link with "outside" after a long hard winter. People waved and shouted greetings to passengers, whether they knew them or not. The captain and his two pilots called out orders to the well-trained crew, while the passengers hustled about collecting their baggage. Dad, with Carlton on his shoulders and Mother beside him, became part of the colourful noisy scene.

Mother's eyes searched for Grandmother. Finally she caught sight of her and observed with a pang how her small figure drooped. From the lines of fatigue in her still-handsome face, Mother knew that the trip had been hard. Grandmother stood at the railing, anxiously scanning the crowd. Holding a large valise in one hand, she kept firm grip with the other on a dark-haired four-year-old whose brown eyes were as big as saucers. Grandmother's face lit up when she saw them, and Mother smiled and waved.

The *Grahame* began to make the river journey regularly after Grandmother's arrival. The new steamboat brought a hundred passengers with each trip, and my parents' hotel was soon filled to capacity. Grandmother's experience managing a cafeteria for a friend in Calgary was a great help. It did not take long for her to size up Annie and come to the same conclusion as Mrs. Stewart: Annie was fine but she would need a firm hand. Ms. Mosquito settled down, knowing that she had met her match, and between them they soon had the place in good order.

All went well until Edward, two years older than Carlton and always starting something, was caught by Annie teasing and pinching him. She grabbed Edward and, eyes blazing, shook him, all the while making dire threats in Cree. The frightened four-year-old screamed for help, bringing the two women running. My grandmother was furious and looked to my mother for support. She, however, decided to stay out of it. Someone had to straighten out that spoiled child, she told us later. My Grandmother's Irish temper was aroused even further and she decided to give Annie a tongue-lashing. The Indian woman did not give her a chance. With a curt, "Yes Ma'am," she picked Carlton up and stalked out, making it plain that when it came to protecting her charge she was on the warpath.

Except for breakfast, the dining room was closed on Sunday, giving my parents a chance to show Grandmother the town and surrounding countryside. Mother detested having to wait on table in her condition, especially as most of the boarders were men. Dad's view was, "It can't be helped, the hotel has been losing money for months and now we have to make up for it." Mother would gladly have changed places with Grandma in the kitchen, but she had neither skill or experience as a cook. Nor could she have stood the heat from the large cookstove. Dad had thrown out one man for snickering at her, and she was proud of him for doing so. Although a good head taller than my father, this smart alec slunk away when Dad pointed to the door and ordered him out. My father was slow to anger, but one look from his piercing eyes that seemed to look right through you, was always enough to send us children cringing to our rooms when we were culprits. It even seemed to work on grown-ups.

One lovely Sunday, a few weeks before my birth, Dad suggested to Mother that she escape the noise and confusion of the hotel and accompany him to the homestead where he wanted to repair the fences. The boys were left playing under the trees beside the hotel. Edward was doing acrobatics on the swing, and Carlton played in the sandbox under Annie's watchful eye while Grandma rested. My parents decided to take Trixie with them. Brownie was left to help guard the boys.

After reaching the cabin, Dad pointed to the far corner of the yard where he would be working within calling distance. Mother decided to rest. With a book in hand, she headed for the small cot in the cabin. But the woods through the open door seemed to beckon to her. She put her book down and walked toward them. Standing at the edge of the clearing, she contemplated the tall trees – untouched except by birds and squirrels, rain and sunlight – the way they had begun in God's mind, tree beside tree, standing at random beneath the blue sky.

Noticing the markings of a trail, she decided to follow it. The trees soon began to thin out allowing the sun to filter through. Ahead, in the bright sunlight, she saw a patch of tall-stemmed wild blue flax swaying in the gentle breeze. Enchanted by this lovely display she picked a few flowers. She stopped to watch birds nesting overhead and laughed when she heard herself confiding aloud that she was nesting too. Mother came to another clearing covered with spikes of lavender fireweed and Indian paintbrush. She had been told that they were the first growth to appear after the earth was scorched by fire. She began picking them and soon had a big bouquet, pleased at how well the scarlet paintbrush blended with the lavender fireweed and blue flax.

When she decided to go back to the cabin, she looked for the path but could find no trace of it. She had been drawn to the flowers and had not realized that the path had petered out. After wandering around, she discovered a faint trail and followed it until it branched off. By this time she had lost all sense of direction and began to panic but, remembering Dad's advice, she decided to sit and wait for him to find her. After resting a while, she placed part of her bouquet on one of the paths and started along it. Within a short distance she was back to the fireweed clearing and realized she had made a full circle. Retracing her steps to the fork, she picked up her flowers and, placing them on the other path, started down it.

There was now a chill in the air and it was getting late. Mother tried to control her fear. The birds had stopped their twittering and even the squirrels were silent. The trees that had earlier looked so stately now seemed to close in on her. Overhead, a black cloud moved rapidly across the sky and she heard the distant rumble of thunder. Adding to her anxiety, my mother now felt a twinge of abdominal pain that stopped her in her tracks. It was followed by a few more. It was not the first time this had happened. At home she would not have been concerned, but out here with a storm brewing she had cause for alarm. Her time was getting close and it was well known that thunderstorms often brought on labour. Dad would be looking for her by now but her heart sank as she remembered his warning of the dangers of the woods. Bear and cougar were often trapped in this vicinity and she had heard of people who died from exposure, for nights were cold here, even at this time of year.

Sinking onto the grass, she sobbed out her fear as well as the frustration and tension that had been building up for months. After a few minutes, she wiped her eyes with her petticoat and realized that she felt better. As always when in trouble, her thoughts turned to her Aunt Em's wise counseling. Mother could almost hear her say, "God is always willing to help us, if we but ask." Calmed by her prayers, she was about to press on when she heard the whirring scold of a squirrel. She smiled up at the small animal. He seemed unafraid. Yet she believed that nature had given her knowledge and instinct far greater than that of any creature of the forest. In a more positive frame of mind, she called out Dad's name as loudly as she could, and then called again and again.

Suddenly, she heard a faint barking. The barking grew louder and she knew it was Trixie. A few minutes later the little dog burst through the undergrowth jumping and licking her face with joy. After a few impatient barks Trixie started off again – slowly enough for Mother to follow him. In a short while they reached the homestead. It was dark in the cabin but, after lighting a candle, she found the note Dad had left on the cot. Secure in the knowledge he had gone to search for her and would soon be back, she drifted off to sleep, exhausted, Trixie at her side. Dad returned soon after, pale-faced, to find her lying there. She was too tired to tell him about her experiences that night but insisted that Trixie be given a special meal. And he was.

I was born on a hot summer day in Grouard's Catholic Mission Hospital, attended by the good sisters and Dr. Boulanger. As Mother's labour pains grew intense, she wondered where everyone was, especially her mother who had come so far to be with her for the occasion. Grandmother, unaware that this second baby would be born in less time than usual, was having a chat with a new friend. Dad was sure Grandma would be with Mother and went to attend to his team, taking along a tin of axle grease to apply to Babe's and Girlie's ears for protection against the tiny gnats brought out by the hot weather. The gnats, mosquitos, and bulldog flies were driving his horses crazy, so that afternoon he set fire to the manure pile beside the barn and left the horses to doze in peace. I had picked an awkward time to be born – high noon, and on a Sunday. Listening to Mother reminisce twenty years later, I got the distinct impression that she and Dad could have managed quite nicely without me. When I mentioned this, Mother quickly changed to a lighter mood, quoting a little poem: "A Child Born on the Sabbath Day / Is Fair and Wise and Good and Gay."

According to Mother, I was my Dad's girl at the start. Although I was a towhead like Carlton, Dad was pleased that my eyes were brown like his. He also got a kick out of my scrappy disposition while protecting my brother. I have an old photo taken when Carlton and I were three and one. In it I am leaning forward, scowling at Dr. Green, the photographer, for making Carlton cry with his horrible faces. Mother was still indignant years later. "We'd waited a year for a photographer, only to have it ruined by a smart alec." Yet I treasure this photo, even if like Carlton and me, it has become a bit battered.

Janet, the Snowball's baby, was born three weeks after I. The two of us caused a bit of good-natured rivalry between our parents – especially our fathers. According to Mother, Janet was slow learning to walk, while I could walk and even climb stairs before I was a year old. Janet cut her first tooth at the age of two months, and I did not have a tooth in my head until I was a year old. Joe would usually start it by looking me over with an astonished expression, saying, "Not a single tooth!" Then while shaking his head, he said, "You know Wilbur, you should have Doc Green make her a false set." Dad retaliated, "If that daughter of yours hasn't learned to walk by the time she's ready for school, Beulah will push her there in her carriage." Our mothers laughed, pretending to be above such nonsense. Although I was a nice plump baby, I did not look nearly as fat as Janet. Grandmother continually pointed this out, saying, "If, like the Snowballs, we had a cow – Beulah would gain weight." Yet Mother remembered, to her satisfaction, the day the doctor had a scale shipped in. "I'll never forget that day we mothers and your Grandmother bundled you both off to be weighed and discovered that you weighed half a pound more than Janet. I wouldn't have traded that half-pound for all the tea in China."

Grouard was now bursting at the seams as more and more people poured into the country. It also brought such examples of outside civilization as the motor car. One day, the mayor, Bob Potts, received delivery of a new Cadillac, causing great excitement. This event was followed by the arrival of two more cars, both Model T Fords, bright red in colour with solid brass trim, and soon people began to complain about the dust and noise as the three cars roared up and down Main Street. However, for the most part, the citizens were proud of this indication of progress, saying that now the rains had let up, the entire length of main street, stretching as far as Buffalo Bay, would make a lovely motor drive after it was smoothed out.

CHAPTER THIRTEEN

Rumours Become Reality

The high hopes the citizens had for Grouard early in 1915 turned into anger and frustration as the railway approached Enilda and it became certain that Grouard would be bypassed. Only a few months before, lots were selling for two thousand dollars and realtors were making a fortune. The steady growth had continued with newcomers arriving as fast as the three boats that plied the river and the lake could bring them in.

Then rumours began to circulate that the Edmonton-Dunvegan and British Columbia Railway intended to bypass Grouard in favour of High Prairie, with the divisional point at Round Lake (now known as McLennan). Although odd bits of information such as this had been surfacing for the past year, my father, along with the rest of the town, had not paid much attention. Grouard, like many small towns, thrived on gossip. While hauling equipment for the railway survey crew, Dad heard confirmation of these rumours. Thoroughly shaken, he decided to keep this news from Mother. He was in enough trouble with her as it was, and as he jolted over the rough trail he knew that he had brought it on himself.

One morning while shaving, he casually mentioned that he had accepted a freighting job. "You're more capable of running this place than I am," he said, as he ran the flat razor over his cheek, while watching Mother's reflected reaction in the washstand mirror.

There was a long silence. When Mother answered she did so in a quiet voice. "But you can't always slough off your responsibilities, Wilbur!" Her eyes blazed as she reminded him of their movie theater and the hotel in Edmonton. She had resisted buying this hotel from the beginning, she said, and she was tired of managing the business while he galloped around the country showing off his precious matched team. Dad had never seen her so angry. He broke into a cold sweat imagining her packing up the kids and heading for Calgary with her mother.

"The honeymoon," my mother sadly reminisced, "was over." But walking out on her husband was not the answer. She had nearly given in to him when she saw the hurt look in his brown eyes. Perhaps he had been a bachelor for too many years to change, and he could not stand being cooped up any more than the lions that he and Frederick had encountered in Africa. But her anger, and the fact that she had two children to consider, stiffened her resolve to stand up to him. The past year had been difficult for Mother, especially the last few months. The coming of spring had brought on a rush of business to the hotel. As well, there had been many sleepless nights walking the floor with a sick baby, while my father slept. The teeth I had been so slow in cutting had come through all at once, according to Mother. "When you finally recovered," she said years later, eyes shining with pleasure, "you never again left me for your father." She was right. I would always be his princess, but I was my mother's girl from then on.

Mother found out about the railway bypass while serving a group of local businessmen one morning. Mother was so startled by a remark she overheard that she almost dropped her tray of coffee. One of the group apparently had not heard the rumour before and kept repeating in a loud voice, "High Prairie! I can't believe anyone can take that seriously." So that was back of Wilbur's latest scheme! Reluctantly, she gave in to the necessity of Dad's freighting job.

When it became certain that Grouard would be bypassed, Frank Oliver, an Edmonton MP and federal cabinet minister, ordered work stopped by way of protest. Grouard businessmen hired surveyors to check out the new route in hopes of finding an excuse for having the decision changed. But it was to no avail. The authorities continued to back the new route, leaving Grouard stranded. The decision brought anger and unhappiness to the townspeople. There had been rumours; still, the news, when it came, was a shock. There were protests, petitions, and delegations – all fruitless, as the selection was not to be altered.

Many felt that the engineering and economic facts did not warrant the decision, and there were dark hints about favouritism and benefits to those who had property along the route. This could well have been true, as there was much of that sort of conniving in the early days of railway building. But there were other factors. The people of Grouard did not understand that the choice of McLennan as a divisional point was based on government law and railway regulations. In the days of steam locomotion the location of divisional points was an important, often crucial, issue. There had to be an adequate supply of good water for the locomotives and a suitable site for the shops, roundhouses and other railway buildings, and the community that would grow up around them.

Mirror Landing, or Smith as it was later renamed, was so far the only divisional point north of Edmonton, and as construction approached the western end of Lesser Slave Lake, it became clear that another location would have to be found for that purpose within the next thirty miles or so. With this in mind, the management sent out a man from Edmonton to scout for a site that met their requirements. In due course this man arrived at Round Lake, saw the large body of water and the level area immediately adjacent to the south shore, and decided this would be just right. Taking a sample of water from the lake, he started his trip home to report. However, he fell in with bad company, got drunk, and when he sobered up found himself in Grouard. He was in a predicament for he had lost the sample of water and, having wasted enough time on his spree, did not want to go back to Round Lake. One of his pals came to his rescue, suggesting he fill another bottle with water from Lesser Slave Lake, saying, "No one will know the difference as the lakes are all the same." This he did, and on his return the water was analyzed, found to be suitable, and thus a strong case was made for selecting McLennan over Grouard.

There was another fact to be taken into account. Some years before, Frank Oliver had the Railway Act amended so that sidings had to be located not more than seven miles apart on the western railways for the convenience of farmers hauling grain with teams. When the railway selected McLennan as the divisional point, it was obvious that an extra twenty-five or thirty miles could not be added to go north to Grouard and back again. High Prairie was the right distance from Enilda, and McLennan was also about seven miles west of Kathleen, the next siding to the east. McLennan won the honour and the railway lost a great deal of money as a result – their new divisional point was without adequate water. Construction on Number 2 Highway commenced within the next few years, following the railway and leaving Grouard even more isolated.

Years later, a former Northern Alberta Railway manager confirmed this story of the lost bottle of water to my husband, Ged, when the two met in High Prairie, where the retired railway man had gone hunting. If the water from the lost bottle had been analyzed, it would have been discovered that the water from Round Lake was quite undrinkable and totally unsuitable for steam engines. Water from Lesser Slave Lake had to be freighted in by water tanks and a large dam was built at McLennan to store it. Today, seventy years later, McLennan is still shipping in water, though now it comes by canal from Lake Winagami.

While the town was still reeling from the shock of being bypassed, news came over the telegraph wires that shocked the entire world. World War I was declared. The German army had invaded France. Within a few months, eighty local men enlisted. Although saddened by their departure, the citizens of Grouard still had serious decisions to make concerning their own future.

Then, over the telegraph wires, came the exciting news to our family that my Uncle Ralph, father's younger brother, was to arrive in a few days. Mother was as delighted as Dad. Having lived next door to the Freelands for so many years, she regarded him as a brother, too.

To their surprise, Uncle Ralph arrived in a Canadian soldier's uniform. Since the United States had shown no indication of becoming involved in the war to that point, Ralph decided to join the Canadian army and, as he wanted to visit them, he had travelled to Edmonton and enlisted there. When the citizens of Grouard learned of this, he and my parents were included in some of the functions being held for their departing servicemen. The biggest event was a gala ball given by the local North West Mounted Police.

Although he was having a wonderful time, Uncle Ralph decided that he would rather spend the rest of his leave with his family. The woods were aflame with autumn colours, and after city life, he loved driving out to the homestead in the clearing in the woods with my parents, who suddenly no longer felt the need to devote so much time to running the hotel.

The rains and hot sun that summer had produced a bumper crop of saskatoon berries. They hung as large as grapes from bushes that encircled the field around the homestead. One day Dad and Ralph, Carlton and Edward at their heels, ate handfuls of them. They made a tasty dessert to go along with Grandma's picnic lunch. Full and content, the men decided to doze in the sun. My mother had other plans. After dumping out the remains of their lunch, she tied the empty lard pails around their waists and, with a determined look, sent them back the bushes. They knew there was no use arguing, and in a short while the pails were filled with the juicy berries.

When Ralph carried the pails of fruit in to Annie, she told him how important this particular berry had been to her people. Her parents were part of a band of Cree who moved their teepees near the fort for convenience and protection. Most of the men were trappers, but a few, her father among them, were buffalo hunters. Their diet consisted mostly of meat. To supply the tribe with food during the winter, the women made pemmican from buffalo meat. The meat was cut into strips, dried, then pounded into a paste with melted fat and saskatoon berries, and pressed into small cakes. It tasted delicious, was highly nutritious, and could be stored for long periods. It was used by fur-traders and travellers to the forts as much as by the Natives. Pemmican was, in fact, widely used by Indians, Métis, and whites.

After we children had been put to bed, Dad basked in Mother's goodwill, while she and Ralph recalled the pranks they had played on one another. Yet, beneath the laughter, they shared the pain of knowing that Ralph would soon be leaving, perhaps never to return. Seventy-two men left Grouard on the same boat as Ralph, including their friend, Dan Hayden.

After Ralph left, great waves of homesickness swept over my mother. She took it so hard that my adventurous father was glad he had not mentioned that he wished he could also have enlisted. Instead, he drove her to their cabin. She wanted to be alone to cry out her frustration and her need for Aunt Em. Exhausted, she fell asleep. Awakening a while later, she splashed her face with cold water and ventured outdoors.

It was evening. The meadowlarks were spilling out their glad songs. While standing there in the twilight, she became one with the sky, the trees, the earth, and felt the joy of the Creator. While looking up at the cloud patterns and then down at the clearing, she seemed to hear a voice saying, "There is a time to look up, and a time to look down." Her faith strengthened, she resolved to hang on, no matter how bad the storm. In His hand, she would place her trust and her destiny.

It was July 1915 and the town of Grouard was practically deserted. My parents had stayed on, hoping to get an offer for their hotel. Dad finally agreed with my mother – the looters were the only ones interested, and they would have the place stripped before they themselves reached the Crossing. This sort of thing had been going on for some time. Even the mile-long sidewalk was being torn up for firewood.

Grandmother and Edward had returned to Calgary a week before. Edward was six now and he was going to school in the fall. The parting was made easier by knowing that the railway was only a few miles from Peace River, where my parents were now determined to go.

Dad whistled nervously as he adjusted the thick ropes that tied their belongings to the wagon and stifled an urge to look up, knowing that his wife was standing at the window above. He would have to be patient. She was three months pregnant again, battling morning sickness, and might even be shedding a few tears. His whistling stopped abruptly and he muttered with a sigh, "I'll never understand women." His glance took in the neatly-packed covered wagon and their four-year-old son holding the reins. He thought Ollie agreed with him that running a hotel was a monotonous job and was looking forward to a new challenge.

Dad was right; he did not understand women, my mother in particular. They were poles apart. She had a practical nature, while he was a man of vision whose instincts had rarely let him down. He did admit that he had been on the wrong track since his return from South Africa, but the pull of the land was so strong that he had no doubts but that they were now heading in the right direction. His first trip to Peace River Crossing had convinced him of this. The land around Peace River was rich and black, he told my mother. He and Sam had dropped off freight at Brick's old mission farm on the Shaftsbury Trail, and they were amazed at the variety and abundance of the crops and vegetables growing there.

He might have been looking years ahead. We have a photo of him standing in a field of oats as high as his shoulders, heads thick and heavy – a bumper crop – grown in our back field behind Misery Mountain, a few miles from the mission on Shaftsbury Trail. We grew acres of sweet corn. The sandy hill beside the house was covered with ripe red tomatoes and cucumbers. Produce such as this could only be grown successfully in such a valley where the sun's rays bounced off the steep hills surrounding it.

My father tried not to compare the new team, Nell and Bess, with his former Clydesdales, though he knew he had made a good trade for Girlie after Babe was gone. Besides a small cash settlement, he had received the team and harness, the covered wagon, a white-faced cow and calf, a dozen hens and a rooster, and Bess's colt. Except for the colt, he had arranged for the livestock to be brought to Peace River in the fall.

Mother never forgot the look of misery in Dad's eyes when he staggered in from an all night vigil with his sick mare, Babe. He had called in William McCue, an expert horseman whose Percheron stallion had also died of swamp fever a year ago. But nothing could save Babe. In her agony before she died, she kicked a hole in the ground deep enough to bury her. Dad, my mother believed, was relieved when the ordeal was finally over He tried not to show his grief, and for this she was grateful, but wished she knew of a way to comfort him. A few nights later, she was awakened by the creaking of a rocking chair coming from the nursery. Slipping out of bed, she opened the door and there was my father looking himself again, as he softly sang his baby to sleep. She too felt comforted as she crept back to bed.

Mother had been anxious to leave Grouard, yet now the time had come an unexplainable sadness came over her. This had been their third venture during the five years of their marriage. Each time they walked away, they not only lost a considerable amount of money but many of their possessions as well. Now with their hotel in Edmonton gone and very little cash, they were moving again. She still believed in Dad, though. He was a dreamer, but a doer as well. His record in South Africa had proven this. After talking it over, my parents agreed that the time spent in Grouard had not been wasted. There was satisfaction in this forced exodus. If nothing else, it separated the get-rich-characters from others like themselves who were prepared to stick it out whatever the cost.

Childish laughter and the creaking of a swing drew Mother to the opposite window of the hotel, and she smiled as she watched the scene below. Beneath a bower of leaves from two poplar trees that Dad had used for posts, Mother caught a glimpse of Ethel McKenzie's blond pigtails, standing straight up as she flew through the air, and me – arms and legs clutching my friend – screaming with delight. Catching a glimpse of two brown arms, Mother sighed with relief. Annie was in charge. Her smile turned to tears at the thought of losing Annie, and she marveled at her change of heart since the first time they met.

Could Annie have changed so much in the past two years? Or had she herself changed? Had she learned to look beneath the surface?

Perhaps Mother's patience had a lot to do with it, but Annie deserved credit too. The long hours and hard work were not easy for this proud woman, born to the freedom of the woods. Yet she had stayed. Stoic that she was, Annie did not allow herself to become emotional while saying good-bye to her small charges. Whispering, "Don't forget your Annie," she hugged us both. It was more difficult saying good-bye to Mother. She had no words, but the look in her dark eyes said it all. Annie would be working at the mission; she knew my parents' recommendation had made this possible.

We were off at last, waving farewell to Annie, who rushed out with our nearly forgotten lunch. When we approached the bridge, Dad handed the reins to Carlton before hopping down to make sure that Bess's colt got safely across. As the outfit trundled over the bridge on the road to a future in the new land to the west, Mother turned back to watch the past fall out of sight.

The beginning of Grouard is in part the story of so many communities of this continent, particularly in Canada. As the map rolled back, from east to west in those early days, it was clear that navigable rivers and lakes played a prominent part. Travel by water was always cheaper, easier, and quicker than the overland struggle. Many people coming north from Edmonton, found the north-west end of Lesser Slave Lake a natural stopping place to rest and prepare for journeys ahead.

Two early traders, Jim Cornwall and Fletcher Bredin, chose that site for their trading post and general store. It was a good choice. The lake was filled with a large variety of fish, as well as being near a heavily wooded area abounding with fur-bearing animals. The post was soon surrounded by Indian teepees and the two young men made a small fortune from the rising price of fur. When the lake level rose twelve feet, a new site was found a little to the west. The town of Grouard ultimately came into being on this location.

In 1879, what started out as the Indian War Trail and later became the Lesser Slave Lake Portage was cleared out, widened, and improved for the Hudson Bay's brigade of ox-drawn Red River carts loaded with furs and goods, as well as supplies sent from Edmonton to be transported from one post to another. Although somewhat improved, the cart road was, according to Somers Somerset, who went over the trail with one of the Bay's brigades, "an oozy swamp of black mud, that never had a chance to dry out, owing to the dense forest." It took early travellers six days to reach the Crossing, with great clouds of mosquitos descending on the animals, as well as the travellers, for most of the trip.

Jim Cornwall's petitions for improving these deplorable conditions finally bore fruit. In 1906, the newly formed Government of Alberta came through with the money and manpower for the Peace River Grouard Trail, as it was referred to by the Public Works Department in Edmonton. It would be called Old Portage for some years, and finally became known as the Peace River Highway, or Number 2 Highway. During the following ten years, a great deal more money and labour was spent on the trail. Bridges and culverts were built and corduroy laid over the worst spots. Dad had been over the trail twice during the summer, with good weather on both occasions. He hoped his luck would hold. They would be spending the first night at John McLeod's canvas hotel in High Prairie.

The day was warm and sunny and the family enjoyed a picnic beside a small creek. They did not tarry long though. If Kate, the colt, did not need to be nursed and rested, they might not have stopped at all. Dad was anxious to keep his rendezvous with Sam, who was to meet them at the hotel.

Mother had not worried about the trip, knowing of the improvements to the road. But the corduroy was worse than she had expected. The poles were not anchored, causing the wagon to lurch as contact was made with the loose wood. When she complained, Dad's comment was, "Be thankful the poles are still in place." He did not dare tell her what had happened to Joe and Alfred Beaudry a couple of summers before, after the rain had washed the logs away. The following is an account of what happened by E. William Marx in *Grouard-Peace River Trail* (High Prairie, AB: author, 1984):

> There wasn't a cloud in the sky when the Beaudry's left Grouard. It was as they were approaching Little Prairie that they noticed the atmosphere had become still and oppressive. Looking up, they saw a mass of great black clouds moving rapidly towards them. They pulled over, and as quickly as possible, set up the tent and got their bedding and grub box inside. They barely had time to unhitch the team and gather firewood, before the clouds opened up with a deluge of rain. It poured all night and on into the morning. They were worried about the pole bridge at Benjamin Creek, near Blackbirds Stopping Place a few miles ahead. The road without ditches looked like a lake, and was practically impossible to travel over; but they had no choice, they had to move on. Once over the bridge, they set up camp on a high ridge. The steady downpour kept them here two days and nights along with thirty other teams, all crowded together on the same ridge. When they were finally able to proceed down the Grouard Hill, the mud and ruts made it unnecessary to lock their back wheels.
>
> Back at Benjamin Creek on their return journey, they found the bridge down stream among the willows. After securing the wagon box to keep it from floating away, they let the team swim across. It was the same situation at Bearhead Creek. With the bridge up on the shore, quite a few people were stranded on both sides. Their only solution was getting together

and pulling the wagons over by hand, after
forcing the horses to swim the turbulent stream.
The South Heart River was another matter.
There, travellers had been waiting three days.
They finally built a raft large enough to hold a
wagon, and poled it across a considerable
distance on water the depth of four feet above
the road. The whole trip took them fifteen days
– covered in mud most of the time. One happy
incident, they remembered, was a freighter
handing out cases of cookies, saying they might
as well eat them as they would get soggy.

Compared to the Beaudry's trip my parents' journey was
uneventful. At High Prairie my parents had a good night's sleep,
and if they had not been informed would never have suspected
the hotel was constructed mostly of canvas. They started off
early next morning, heading through town to the corduroy road
beyond.

My mother had watched many of Grouard's buildings being
torn down and dragged away. Still, she was not prepared to see
so many familiar establishments operating as if they had always
been in High Prairie. These included Thompson's Hardware,
Sid Smith's Mercantile, Brown's Livery Stable, Gregary's
Grocery, the post office, and a grain elevator in the process of
being rebuilt. As Dad said, "If the railway won't go to Grouard,
then Grouard will go to the railway."

Everything was closed at this early hour, but as they were
passing Sid Smith's store they noticed that his door was open.
Recognizing Dad, he came to the door. Business was good, he
said, in answer to Dad's enquiry. The train made a difference,
bringing in new settlers as well as trade to this already well-
settled district.

"I was sorry to hear of the loss of your Clydesdale mare,"
Sid said. "That's a good sturdy team you've replaced them with,
though."

Dad nodded, "I'll never come close to owning another team

to match Babe and Girlie." Then in a cheerful voice, as he slapped the reins on the horses' rumps, "This team is a lot faster though, even with the colt."

As they made their way over the rough street with its muddy low spots, my mother wondered why more rain seemed to fall in this area than elsewhere. There was a particularly deep hole where the logs began. Sam, who knew every stretch of corduroy and pothole on Old Portage, was waiting when they pulled up, and a few more inexperienced drivers soon came along. After looking it over, both men agreed that part of the load would have to be removed. Mother watched them struggle through the mud with the heavy cookstove, amazed at their strength. Neither was very tall, nor had they an ounce to spare, yet they handled it with ease.

Bess and Nell were now able to make it through, but Kate refused to budge. All the pushing and pulling, even the whinnying of the mare, could not persuade her. They finally decided to carry her across, but first they would need to protect themselves from her sharp hooves. While the men searched for ropes, Mother suggested they lend Kate their gum boots, then she would not mind the mud. She got her laugh as well as a threat that they would throw her in if there were any more wisecracks.

It was lunch time for the colt when she was safe again with her mother. The men were not as lucky. They still had to reload the rig, and with a mudhole at the other end of the corduroy it meant doing it all over again.

Before they could get started, a cloud of hungry mosquitos descended on everyone. The men hurried to get out the axle grease to protect the horses' ears and noses, while Mother looked for the citronella to protect us. The bush began to thin out as they approached the end of the corduroy, allowing the breeze to blow the insects away.

At last they were through and we all trooped across the meadow to a small pond. Carlton and I were allowed to wade, while the men washed the mud off their hands and boots. Mother said later that, although she would not admit it at the time, she did wonder while unpacking the lunch where she could have got the idea that freighting was an exciting life. It was just plain difficult.

As Sam started back over the corduroy to where he had left his team, he hesitated and with an apologetic look said, "I hope you both understand that I'd rather go along with you. It's just that I feel responsible for these young people who might never make it on their own."

Dad agreed that assisting the others waiting to cross was just as well. "We will need a couple of days head start, as we intend to take it easy."

"On account of the children," Mother added, blushing slightly.

"And don't forget the colt," Sam said, with a mischievous grin.

CHAPTER FOURTEEN

Saskatoon Birthday Pie

Sometime later, while in that blissful state between sleep and consciousness, Mother looked about her, wondering what could have awakened her. Then she heard a sound, the shrill twitter of a bird from a tree overhead. Through the silence she heard the querulous, sleepy chirps of fledglings. She smiled, thinking of her own little ones sleeping soundly in their corner. Overcome by weariness, she sank back on her soft mattress and was soon asleep again.

She awoke to the miracle of a new day that gathered and grew as night crept off before the whispering dawn. A band of purest white, high as the morning star, faded into a silvery mist caught by the lightest clouds, giving them a brilliant glow of saffron, scarlet, and amethyst. Letting out a breath she had not known she was holding, Mother tried to capture the magic of moments ago.

She was startled when Dad reached out and helped her back under the covers, "I haven't seen anything like it since leaving South Africa," he said. Then with a smile in his voice added, "I believe you're beginning to like this gypsy life, now that the trip is nearly over."

Mother agreed that there had been good times. "But you have to admit, Wilbur, we were lucky. If it had rained we could have been stuck in the mud for ages with mosquitoes eating us alive. It would have also prevented me from walking, and I could never have endured jolting over the rough trail. We should have taken Sam's advice and left in March when the snow covered the ruts. I was not pregnant then. But you had to haul freight with Sam." From his rueful expression she realized that he had been too preoccupied to be aware of her problems. She relented, "Except for being weary, I feel wonderful and the beauty of the sunrise is a good omen."

Knowing that she was right about taking Sam's advice, he was happy to agree. "We should sleep awhile longer, Ollie, we've a long day ahead of us." He soon drifted off, but for Mother sleep was not to return that day. She pondered how married life had changed her – more, perhaps, than it had her husband. She felt she had matured and become protective of her husband as well as her children. But she was learning, she thought with some amusement, never to let on that "himself" was not in charge. Her mind wandered back over events of the trip.

After leaving Sam that first day, they had continued over the rough corduroy road with its pole bridges every few miles. Worried for fear the jolting would bring on a miscarriage, Mother decided to walk behind the wagon through the roughest places, often with Carlton beside her.

He was not quite four, yet showed signs of becoming a good woodsman, pointing out a squirrel or chipmunk half hidden behind a leaf or branch. Like his father, he already had a way with animals. Feeling sorry for Kate that first day, he sneaked some sugar lumps and let her nuzzle them out of his hand. After that, she followed him everywhere – even through mud holes and over the wobbly corduroy. This was a help to Dad. The colt could have held them up if she had repeated that first performance.

Discussing the trip with Carlton many years later, I mentioned that I remembered Nell and Bess, but did not remember the colt. "I'm not surprised," he commented dryly, "You were only two at the time and Kate grew up faster than you." I laughed with the realization that the colt was the same gentle Kate I had been riding back and forth to town since I was ten. Only on special occasions though, for she had already put in her day's work, my dad would grudgingly remind me as he adjusted the stirrups. "It's a long way for a taffy pull, Princess," he said as he helped me into the saddle. Then relenting a little, he told me to have a good time and be home early. Kate did not seem to mind. She perked up her ears as I sang lustily while we plodded through the jackpines.

Nothing pleased my father more than being up before the dew was off the grass on a beautiful morning. According to Mother, he had a fire lit and breakfast started before we were awake. Hours later, when the sun had climbed in the sky and he found himself nodding off, he knew it was time for us to have a rest. He pulled the team off the road and erected the pup tent where we rested during the heat of the day. This way we could carry on until late evening. With so much freight passing over the trail, stopping houses were appearing every few miles. This was to my parents' advantage, as they needed a clearing for their tent. Dad had met many of the owners while freighting and was always given a friendly welcome.

As the heavy timber thinned out, we emerged into a more lightly wooded area with small open meadows covered with grass and hay. Now that the roads had improved, Carlton was allowed to drive giving Dad a chance to stretch his legs, and at last I could join the walkers, although I was probably carried on Dad's shoulders most of the time. Knowing the route, my father usually managed to get us near one of the small lakes or sloughs that dotted the meadows. We children, Kate following, delighted in wading among the bullrushes while Mother soaked her swollen feet. Dad unharnessed the team and fastened small bells to their halters – a trick he had learned from his fellow freighters. It not only alerted him of their whereabouts, but also frightened off bears, wolves, or other marauders of the night. After a good rest, we were on our way again.

We crossed Bearhead Creek near Little Prairie and approached Benjamin Creek. Dad pointed out an area to the north to Mother. "That area is known as the Hudson's Bay cattle sheds. The Company sheltered as many as thirty oxen there during the winter because of the abundance of wild hay and a good supply of fresh water." Mother enjoyed sitting beside Dad while he told her what he knew of the history of the country through which they were passing.

Alexander Mackenzie wrote in his diary that he first learned of a trail between Peace River Crossing and Lesser Slave Lake during the winter of 1793, while planning his overland trip with his voyageurs at Fort York.

> The Indians informed me that they had been to hunt at a large lake, called by the Knisteneaux, the Slave Lake .... It is well known to the Knisteneaux who are among the inhabitants of the plains on the banks of the Saskatchiwine River; formerly, when they used to make war in this country, they came in their canoes to that lake and left them there; from thence there is a beaten path all the way to the Fork, or East branch of this river, which was their war road.

He then drew the trail on a map he was producing of the district, along with the above information, naming it the Knisteneaux War Road. Mother said that she could almost see the warriors, resplendent with war paint, slipping silently through the foliage.

My parents made good time, arriving at the Benjamin Creek Stopping Place two days before my birthday. Owned by Louis Courtereille, it was considered by Dad a good choice for celebrating. "We are in luck," Dad quietly told Mother. "That handsome man in the yard is Courtereille, the Métis called Blackbird, the owner of this place."

"Now I understand," Mother whispered to Dad, trying not to smile. "He's called Blackbird because of his big black mustache."

When Dad explained their situation to Blackbird, he agreed to let them use his land for a few days. Calling to his brother-in-law, Joe, they led my parents to a perfect place, in the shelter of a clump of willows near the creek. "In a few weeks," Blackbird said, "there will be many teepees camped along the creek. Friends and relatives come from many miles to help with the haying. Afterwards we travel into thick timber, not far from Reno. There the ground is covered with low bush cranberries and blueberries that grow thick as fleas on a dog's back." He was too dignified to laugh, but his pleasure as he anticipated the happy times ahead shone in his dark eyes.

With Joe's help, the big tent was soon up and the cooking range placed under the front awning. Mother smiled, "I'll need it for baking and cooking the birthday dinner." She and Annie had preserved jars of jellied chicken and fruit. These, and the fresh vegetables Blackbird offered, would make a feast. Mother confessed that she had been worrying about making the birthday cake, when Dad came back from watering the horses with a hatful of ripe, juicy saskatoons. He said with a smile, "Why bother with a cake, Ollie, when you make such delicious saskatoon pie?" Mother laughed, saying she could almost make them in her sleep. With berries for the picking, we always had saskatoon pie on our menu.

They also needed the range to heat water for washing their hair and for their baths, and, with two days' grace, she hoped to have time to wash our clothes. Mother planned to have us all clean and beautiful before Sam and the Brodys arrived. She thought of the little white dress all trimmed with lace that she and my grandmother had made for me. They had even managed a new outfit for Carlton.

"Looking back" – Mother's eyes always lit up when she remembered this event – "the grown-ups had more fun than you children. It's hard to remember what made the affair so special. Perhaps we were really celebrating our new future. We were happy to have Sam with us again, and we met two wonderful people, Anne and Jim Brody, who became our friends." The latter made a hit with me by fashioning a little chair out of clothes pins, just the right size for my mother's present, a tiny doll.

I never tired of hearing her tell this story. I have always felt that celebrating my second birthday along Old Portage Trail, with saskatoon pie instead of birthday cake, was very special.

A few days later, Mother looked up and laughed at the sign pointing back to Grouard, as we approached the hill overlooking Peace River Crossing. It advised travellers to choose their rut with care. They would be in it for some time! We camped that last night near a stopping place called Four Mile Corner in order to get an early start down the treacherous Grouard Hill that led down to the mighty Peace.

Mother gazed down into the beautiful valley below and knew that it had all been worth it. They had reached their promised land. Perhaps it was well that she could not see what lay ahead in time. There would be hardship and sorrow as well as happiness before she was laid to rest beside my father on the first knoll of Misery Mountain. For now, with her little ones beside her and her husband looking across the valley of the town to the rich land beyond, she was content.

CHAPTER FIFTEEN

A Tent for the Winter

I often wonder now, as I fly into Peace River, what I as a little child of two thought when held aloft by my father to view the valley for the first time. It must have looked like fairyland after the long trip through the bush. Perhaps a far memory still exists, for I often feel a sense of wonder as the small plane, slipping downward through the sunlit sky, tilts as it turns towards the airport, bringing the sandbar and the islands breathtakingly close. Looking a few miles upriver from the town, I get a glimpse of a high point of land. Below, the turbulent Smoky, a large river in its own right, empties its waters into the Peace, widening it considerably as it curves towards the north. The high ridge is known as Mackenzie's Outlook, where Alexander Mackenzie's people watched for his return from his historic overland trip to the Pacific Ocean.

On the day of my parents' arrival, the little town sprawled along the river bank nearly a thousand feet below them. Dad pointed to the left, saying that behind the hill a six-hundred-forty-foot trestle bridge was being built in order to bring the railway into town.

Her first look down the steep grade of the Grouard Hill was truly frightening, Mother remembered later. Dad looked worried too as he set to work rough-locking the back wheels of the wagon. This was done by running a chain through the spokes of the back wheels and fastening them to the long pole that extended under the wagon. He knew that even these precautions could fail if the chains were to give way. Telling Mother that most passengers preferred to walk, Dad was relieved when she decided to do the same. On other trips he had relied on his strong Clydesdales; this was the first run for his new team.

He was ready to go when a rig pulled up and two teen-aged boys jumped down, followed by their parents. John and Edith Anderson introduced themselves and their sons, Gordon and Allen. They too had come because of land. After helping rough-lock John's wagon, Dad was off, calling over his shoulder, "If I make it down in one piece, I'll show you a good place to pitch your tent."

Holding the horses back with all his strength, he headed the team down the steep hill, wheels kicking up a cloud of dust as they hugged the curve, coming dangerously close to the edge. When Dad got to the bottom of the two-mile hill, both he and his team were soaking wet. He pulled them off the road and after a brief rest rubbed them down with a gunny sack.

John pulled up beside him, saying as he mopped his streaming face, "That's sure one bear-cat of a hill."

While waiting for their families to walk down, they discussed the town. John was surprised to learn that the population, according to the 1914 census, was around seven hundred people. "Only seven hundred?" he exclaimed. "Why, Grouard had a population of nearly four thousand, a year ago."

"Yes," my father agreed, "but the fact is that there were only two thousand people in the entire Peace River Country in 1911, including what was left of the mighty Beaver tribe." My father told John that this bountiful country with its twenty-five thousand square miles of arable farm land would have been snatched up long ago by white settlers if it had not been so inaccessible.

For the men waiting below, it seemed that their families were taking a long time walking down the long grade. This was not surprising, considering the breathtaking view around every curve. Besides, Gordon, who was carrying me, needed to rest now and then. The women, confined to the cramped quarters of a wagon, were enjoying the freedom of this short interval and getting acquainted with one another.

The site Dad chose for their tents was near the old boat landing, not far from where the flour mill and grain elevator later stood for many years. They were lucky, he said, to find a good spot. This time last year it would have been impossible. Settlers were arriving at such a rate that almost overnight a community of tents appeared along the east side of Main Street. There followed restaurants, shops, a pool hall, a Methodist church, and even a barbershop with a female barber. The outbreak of war, Dad thought, was mainly responsible for the slowdown.

The men soon had the Anderson's tent up and were off for the lumber Dad needed for the floor of our tent. Unlike our friends, we would be living in it until spring. Dad had been told that, with a banking of snow and an insulation of ice from the freezing rain, the tent could be kept warm during the coldest weather.

With John's expertise and help from the two boys, they soon had the floor laid, the canvas up, and everything in place. The Andersons admired the big tent and its isinglass window that let in the sunlight. But it was the wide awning, stretching ten feet down the front, that my parents appreciated most.

Where to put the cookstove was a bit of a dilemma for my mother. She finally decided to have it put under the awning, taking a chance with the weather rather than sleeping in a hot tent all summer. This made it more convenient for heating the "running water," as she jokingly called the water my father hauled by the bucket from the river. It was fun having our meals under the awning while watching the boats ply the waters of the Peace. This was summer, and in summer life expanded with the sunshine.

My father was anxious by now to contact H.A. George, a local farmer and businessman, who had offered Dad a job. Dad had very little cash after paying for Grandmother's and Edward's fare and hoped something would turn up soon. Within the first days of their arrival, Dad drove up the hill and made a deal with

Mr. George to manage his diary farm. He awoke the next day in a cheerful mood. He was up early cooking a big breakfast for the Andersons and us.

This was his way of showing his appreciation for their help. Not only had they helped with the tent, they had offered to mind Carlton and me while he showed Mother the town. For once they were on their way with no encumbrances – we were so intent on our new project, trying to teach Kate to lead, aided by a small rope halter made by Gordon and his father, we did not even hear them drive off.

They had not gone far on their tour of Peace River, when Dad pointed out a charming little log church with a shingled roof and belfry. This was the St. James Anglican Church, whose minister, until recently, had been the Rev. Robert Holmes. Six months later, when my brother John Wilbur was christened here, my parents were to meet this dedicated man and his wife, as well as Captain Magar's attractive Siwash wife, who not only played the organ but was an enchanting soloist. A short distance away was the home of the popular Capt. John Gullion, known for his feats of strength. He had been the builder and captain of the Hudson Bay Company's *Peace River,* the first steamboat to ply the mighty Peace.

Main Street ran east and west in those days. This direct route from Grouard Hill was an asset for freighters bringing in freight to the pier. The town itself had mainly grown without plan, starting as a settlement along the west bank of the river, north of Alexander Mckenzie's fur-trading post, St. Mary's.

Mother was delighted to accept Mr. George's invitation for dinner and a tour of his new Peace Hotel. The impressive three-storeyed building had a dining room with a seating capacity of around one hundred. It was equipped with electric lights and a bathroom with running water and a flush toilet. They were told that the use of the bathroom was free for the ten best rooms which rented for one dollar a night, as well as the eight rooms over the pool hall which rented for fifty cents a night. The public were not forgotten. They were allowed to rent the bathroom for the small sum of fifteen cents.

H.A. George, an employee of the Hudson's Bay Company, was sent to the Crossing in 1901, as factor and manager of the new post. From the time the first settlers arrived, he led the way in most civic affairs – the schools, the first agriculture fair, the hospital, and countless other endeavours. He believed that a great deal of oil could be found in this country, and for years he had an old-fashioned drilling rig operating on top of the George Hill. He studied many books to back up his theory and invested a great deal of time and money in the project which became a reality after his death.

Dad pointed out H.A. George's large four-bedroom town house. The downstairs was mainly one big room that had been used as a ballroom during the years when he was a factor. According to Jean Cameron Kelley who, along with H.A. and two others, left Edmonton on December 26, 1913, in the first car to make it over the trail, it was also used for a classroom. She said that she taught in it during the day, and at night for the first few weeks she slept on her bedroll on the floor behind the stove until a bedroom was available to her. The classroom was still used for parties and dances, usually with Jean at the piano accompanied by any fiddler who might happen along.

The next building of interest was the Royal Bank of Canada, a large two-storey building with living quarters and a balcony on the second floor. The manager was William Stewart, whose wife Susan had been kind to Mother when she first arrived in Grouard. Mrs. Stewart had a beautiful contralto voice and led the way in the many stage productions for which Peace River became noted.

Across the street, on a northeast corner, stood a modern two-storey cafe owned by the Nagles who had also moved here from Grouard. Ma Nagle, like Mother, loved dogs. It was not unusual to see this stout little lady, ambling through the streets with a duck-like walk, surrounded by several dogs. According to local resident Glen Murphy, their St. Bernard, Mutt, often showed up for handouts and afterwards would doze in the sun, taking up most of the sidewalk. One day an irate townsman confronted Ma, saying that Mutt had bitten him and that he was taking the owner to court. Mrs. Nagle claimed to be the owner and during the proceedings asked the man where he had been bitten. He made a motion to his buttocks, and Mrs. Nagle said, "Show me," which he refused to do. Mrs. Nagle then said, "If you can't show me where he bit you, then he didn't bite you." The man threw up his hands and withdrew the charge.

The new Telegraph Office was to the east and up a few steps. The telegrapher, Pierre Grauvreau, was very popular with his hot-off-the-wire news that he made available to all – the only link with the outside world in those war years. Further east stood the Revillon Frères Trading Post, and across the road were a pool hall and stopping places.

The Hudson's Bay Post, later called the Campsall Block, was situated across the street from the new Peace Hotel, and next to it was the new Bank of Commerce. H.A. George had built the first Peace Hotel. Like the stopping houses, the upstairs was one big room, where guests spread their bedrolls on the floor. The room was also used for political meetings and other civic affairs. Cephas Northey set up Peace River's first barbershop on the first floor which he shared with a pool table. It was along here, too, that Bert Hopps built his Empire Theatre, a building that was to serve many uses, one of which was as a court house when the occasion arose. Across the street were a hardware store, a blacksmith shop, and a livery stable. Further south, Dad pointed out two old buildings that had originally been the warehouses built by J. K. Cornwall and Fletcher Bredin. On the other side of the Heart Bridge and to the right before reaching the ferry tower, they passed a few more business places, including a rooming house.

On a high bank near the junction of the Smoky and the Peace, Mother noticed a weather-beaten fence that enclosed a group of small, peaked-roof houses. This area was the burial ground for Indian children. The small houses, according to Mr. George, were attributed to an old belief that as long as the body remained intact, the soul would hover over its old home – the small houses were to keep them intact as long as possible. Directly below was a row of desolate tents and shacks dubbed

Rotten Row. It was a scene that Mother never forgot.

Dad intended to take Mother out to a homestead he was considering beyond the George farm on the other side of the Peace River. The ferry was a new experience for Mother, and looking over the small craft with its wobbly planks, she decided to walk on board instead. Having resumed her comfortable seat in the democrat that went with Dad's job, she became aware of the five hills that completely surrounded the valley. As they were nearing the centre of the river, she was able to make out the faint markings of the white picket fence at the top of Grouard Hill behind them. She was informed by Dad that this was the grave of Twelve-Foot Davis.

Henry Fuller Davis, a native of Vermont, entered the Caribou gold fields at the age of twenty-nine. He laid claim to a twelve-foot strip of land between two contesting companies. It is said that he mined from $10,000 to $20,000 from that claim, earning the nickname Twelve-Foot Davis.

He gave up mining and put his money into various posts including Dunvegan, Peace River, and Fort Vermilion. Not only did he adhere to the Law of the North, leaving his door unlatched along with a supply of food and firewood, but he also helped many get started. He explained it this way: "Them fellers need a kind word as well as a grubstake, and I've got plenty of both." This sort of help was against the policy of the Bay, which discouraged these adventurers, fearing they might later turn to farming and eventually ruin the fur trade. Davis' reputation among the Indians was that of a man to be trusted. With the keen rivalry among fur traders in those days, this was not always the case. According to Reverend Garrioch, Davis was a fine Christian gentleman, although he did not attend church. He probably felt that the great outdoors was his cathedral.

Davis and Jim Cornwall were good friends and whenever they were both at the Crossing they climbed the long Grouard Hill and admired the view. It was also a good lookout for boats returning with furs and supplies. On one occasion, Davis was so overcome by the beauty of the scene, he expressed a wish to be buried on this majestic point overlooking the two rivers. In 1910, Peace River Jim made good his promise and brought his friend's body from Buffalo Bay, where he died, to be buried on that chosen spot. On Davis' tombstone is the following inscription: "Blazer, trader, trapper; he was every man's friend and never locked his cabin door." His fame has grown and a monument has been erected in his honor. Peace River is often called The Land of Twelve-Foot Davis.

• • •

Across the river Mother and Dad entered the village of West Peace River. As they climbed the gentle slope, Mother remembered catching a glimpse of the little hamlet from the top of Grouard Hill. "What a lovely setting!" she exclaimed. "The sun filtering through the trees makes the windows sparkle like diamonds."

Close up, however, the street lost its charm. Dad noted her disappointment and realized she was seeing it through the eyes of a city girl. He decided to fill her in on the history of this settlement that extended along the Shaftsbury Trail as far as Brick's Hill.

According to H.A. George, there was not much there before the 1820s. Then, St. Mary's House made its third and final move to this area, and the village of West Peace River became the fur trading centre for many years. As Mother listened to Dad, the streets seemed no longer a hodge-podge of buildings, but a bustling fur trading centre. The wide river at their feet came alive with colourful canoes, heading for St. Mary's with their cargo of furs. At its peak, five hundred people lived here, mostly Métis and Indians. The announcement of the eighteen-hundred-foot Railway Bridge, as well as the outbreak of the war, was responsible for its decline.

The fourteen shops and businesses that were left seemed to be doing well. Dad pointed out Levesque's Blue Store, a duplicate of the one in Grouard. Twist's Cafe reminded them that it was time for lunch, but on entering they found all the tables taken. It was then that a young man caught Dad's eye and motioned them over, introducing himself as Bill Andrews, the owner of the blacksmith shop they had just passed.

They were soon learning about each other's past. Bill left his native Collingwood, Ontario, bound for Edmonton in 1913. He worked there for a time before buying a horse and saddle. He then travelled with his outfit as far as Mirror Landing on the Edmonton, Dunvegan and British Columbia Railroad, the ED &BCR, riding his horse the rest of the way to Peace River. He arrived in March 1914. After working a year, he had earned enough money to set himself up with modern equipment. "Luck has been with me," he said, "but it won't be for long, if I don't get a move on. I've been hired to do the iron work on the *D. A. Thomas,* couple of blocks up river." As he was leaving, he called over his shoulder, "You should have a look; there won't be another one like it."

He was right. The huge craft being built on a sloping bank was 161.9 feet long, 37 feet wide, and 90 feet from the top of her twin stacks to the bottom of her keel. She was not only the queen of the Peace River but the largest inland boat in Canada. Like the rest, she was a woodburner, but the farsighted owner, Lord Rhonda, had her designed with four heavy oil tanks in her hull, with the hope that they would someday be filled with Peace River oil, instead of having the inconvenience to the crew of foraging for wood. Like his friend H.A. George, Lord Rhonda – or D.A. Thomas as he preferred being called – had enough faith in this country to send a party to survey it, from Athabasca to Fort Chipewyan and north to Fort Smith. Apart from his oil interest, he owned the Diamond P Store and another boat on the Peace called the *Lady Mackworth.*

It is not likely that this Welsh coal king could have been aware of the unique pleasure wood loading excursions gave to the local citizens when they were allowed, for a small fee, to board the *D. A. Thomas* for a picnic, while the crew loaded on wood. My parents did not attend the first picnic, held on July 1, 1916, but according to the Peace River *Record* it was a great success. The boat filled to capacity, as people came from near and far for the opportunity of even a short ride on this renowned steamer. The *D. A.* was to take them down river, fifteen miles to the oil well on Tar Island, before returning to Shaftsbury for their picnic. It was a gay scene, as they tripped up the gangplank to the lively tunes of "McNamara's Band." The orchestra – R.A. McLeod, J.W. Doherty, Larry Jensen, Jimmy Connell, and William McIlroy – showed ingenuity as well as remarkable talent at the local dances. (On one occasion their shenanigans got out of hand. A member was to hit McLeod lightly on the head with a shillelagh as they marched off but got carried away. In his enthusiasm he hit too hard, knocking the poor man out cold.)

My parents stopped for a while, and watched the boat building activity with interest. They finally spotted Bill at work on the keel. He waved his "toasting iron" and they waved back. They did not tarry long and were soon up the steep rise that joined Deacon Hill to Shaftsbury Trail. When they reached the top of the rise, Dad stopped the team while they gazed at the river and island below. Mother thought it was beautiful. Dad agreed but having seen it before said, "I'll bet the view from the top is better." It looked pretty steep but she was game to try the climb. When they reached the main hill, they noticed wide paths encircling it. Dad figured they must be trails made by the buffalo that once roamed these hills.

According to Colin Campbell's journal, these great shaggy beasts had disappeared from the area by 1880. The severe winters and deep snow caused many to die of starvation. Others were killed off by hunters. Approaching the animals on snowshoes, they easily slaughtered as many as fifty-three with their long knives. Small family groups of buffalo found sanctuary in the hills and wooded coulees, and the odd buffalo was still seen as late as 1906. But never again would great herds be seen on Misery Mountain, or grazing along the valleys of the Peace.

My parents did not climb all the way to the top of Deacon Hill – just far enough for a good view of the Smoky and the Peace. Noticing that she looked pale during the climb, Dad steered Mother towards a bluff of trees. She sank down on the grassy knoll with a grateful sigh. It was a hot day, and although she did not show it, she was expecting her third child. They would not go further up the Shaftsbury Trail that day. Instead, they decided to drive to H.A.'s farm. It was a pleasant drive. The scent of silver sage mingled with the fragrance of the odd wild rose bush that still bloomed along the roadside.

Mother realized now that Dad had not taken on an easy job. He explained that after delivering the milk, he would leave the team at the farm every day as they needed the pasture. In the winter he would need the use of the barn. This meant getting up at the crack of dawn, walking through town, crossing on the ferry, and hiking on up the rise that led to the Jack Pine Flats after skirting the little village. Another mile or so, and he would have to climb the long steep George Hill to the farm that was the original homestead of H.A. George.

"The pay isn't great," he admitted, "a dollar a day and feed for the team, as well as for the cow, calf, and chickens that will be arriving in the fall."

"We could almost live off that," Mother said.

George had mentioned to Dad that there would be beef and pork for them after the fall butchering and wild game that his Indian and Métis friends often brought in. Dad went on to say that H.A.'s garden could yield enough for them all. Mother said it sounded fine but wondered about their future needs. Dad had already discussed this with Mr. George who said that after the summer work was finished, he would help Dad find a part-time job, perhaps on the construction of the bridge. Wages were bound to be good. He hoped, Dad said wistfully, that come May they should have enough saved to move to the homestead.

Mr. George was at home and delighted to see them. He insisted on making them tea, while Dad showed Mother the garden and introduced her to the six cows he would soon be milking. Mother did not drink tea, but gladly accepted a glass of cold milk served with delicious cookies. They had been baked, he said, by Miss Helps, a friend of Grandmother's from Grouard, now the chief cook for his new Peace Hotel.

Dad told H.A. that he had intended driving Mother to the

old Anglican Mission farm to meet Allie Brick, but decided they would wait until they could take the children. Mother asked their host if he could tell them a bit more of this man who had made such an impression on her husband, but first she wanted to hear more about H.A. himself.

They learned that although he raised four of the six children by his first wife and had acquired a great deal of property and wealth, he had had more than his share of sorrow. Their oldest son, Max, died at the age of ten and, four months later they had suffered the loss of their two-year-old daughter, Irene. It was only four months since his wife had died. Then the subject turned to Allie Brick.

Mr. George started off saying, "I agree that T.A. Brick, called Allie, is the oldest pioneer in the Peace district. He came west around 1885 to help his father, Rev. J. G. Brick build his Anglican mission farm, first at Old Wives Lake, and later at Shaftsbury, the name he gave the settlement. With ingenuity and a great deal of determination, they managed to protect the first crops from early frosts that hung over the valley those first years. To accomplish this, they invented a game called 'Fort,' involving the Indian school children. Together, they erected clay walls four feet high around the small twelve-acre field. When there was danger of frost, they had great fun building fires with the reward going to the side that produced the most smoke. That plot produced forty-seven bushels of wheat to the acre.

"The following year, Allie travelled to Grouard by ox team with some of their wheat. He sold all the wheat, except two bags, to the Hudson's Bay. The two bags he took to Edmonton by dog team and delivered to representatives of the government. The grain was eventually sent to the Chicago Exhibition of 1893, where it won the World No. 1 Wheat Championship.

"Allie brought in the first threshing machine to the area, and with his neighbour, William Carson, became involved in grain farming. Allie Brick also had a fling at fur-trading, along with other pursuits, and spent two winters with Twelve-Foot Davis, before he returned to his Shaftsbury farm."

In 1906, because of an irregularity, an unscheduled

provincial election had to be called. Brick's neighbors decided that he should represent them. He was nominated by a few settlers, mostly Natives, at a meeting held along the river bank, and on February 15, 1906, was elected over Jim Cornwall with a total vote of eight. His constituency covered one third of Alberta, extending from south of Grande Prairie to the northern tip of the province.

Long after the opening of Alberta's legislature and all the pomp and splendor of the event had faded into the past, the sensation caused by Allie Brick as he made his way down Jasper Avenue would be remembered. Behind his smart team and cutter were several freight rigs in tow; as he was making the long trip overland, he had decided to combine business with his new career. But what caused the sensation that was talked about for years in the North Country were two shaggy-coated, long-eared moose cavorting along, behind the procession, or beside Allie's team. These huge beasts, while contentedly wintering in his barnyard, had formed an attachment to his team of greys, and decided to join this new venture.

CHAPTER SIXTEEN

Northern Justice Gone Awry

Before leaving H.A. George, Mother thanked their host, but she need not have said a word – her enjoyment of his stories shone through her eyes. They caught the ferry and were soon back in camp. Jean put them at ease about us, saying we had been trouble; I had slept all afternoon while the boys played. When she saw the vegetables from H.A.'s garden, Jean was delighted, saying, "It's just what I need for my beef stew."

As they were finishing their meal, Sam arrived full of excitement, saying, "There's been a murder in Jack Pine Flats! Harold Smith has just been shot and Ralph Bradley has given himself up." Both Dad and Sam knew Bradley; they met while delivering freight to Levesque's store.

My parents looked at one another in astonishment. Dad said, "We just drove through there and didn't meet a soul."

The affair involved Bradley's pretty wife, Edith, and the handsome Harold Smith. She had left Ralph Bradley and moved in with Harold and his family. Raging with frustration and jealousy since, Bradley had secured local support by letting off steam to Blair, the barber, and his customers, knowing it would not be long before the entire town knew about his outraged-husband situation.

Just before six o'clock that evening, Harold and his father, W. E. Smith, were making their way through Jack Pine Flats.

According to Mr. Smith's account, they suddenly saw a man advancing on foot toward them. Startled, the older man looked up, saying, "That's Bradley coming at us." Harold did not reply, nor did Bradley say anything.

Mr. Smith's evidence, as given to the police, was that just as the rig drew opposite Ralph Bradley, Bradley reached into his pocket with his right hand. Recalling that Bradley had earlier attempted to borrow a gun and fearful he might now be armed, the father rose from his seat in an attempt to jump out and stop him. But in his haste and anxiety he tripped over the reins and buggy whip, caught his knee on a bolt in the dashboard, and fell across Harold landing heavily on the ground face down. He recollected that as he fell, his son brought the team to a stop and stood up, but he too lost his balance and crashed to the earth just in front of Bradley.

Harold was scrambling to his feet when Bradley shot at him twice with the pistol. The younger Smith began to move towards Bradley, who shot again. This time Harold fell still. In fear and anger, the father got up off the ground to go for Bradley, who threatened him with the gun, saying, "Don't, or I'll get you too." Then as Harold lay motionless, Ralph Bradley walked up to him and deliberately fired two more shots into his body, after which he coolly turned and went towards town, without uttering another word. According to Smith's testimony, the entire encounter lasted only a few minutes.

The postmortem revealed four bullet wounds in Harold's body, two of which would have caused death. The locations were consistent with their having been fired point-blank into Harold Smith as he lay on the ground. Bradley did not give evidence at the preliminary hearing, but he was a witness on his own behalf at the jury trial. He swore he saw a rig approaching and just as it began to pass him the Smiths leapt out, bent on attack. He did admit that their only weapon was a buggy whip. As they advanced, Bradley said he pulled out his pistol and fired one warning shot into the air. Harold did not stop and, as he came closer, he shot four more times in self defence.

After reloading his gun, Bradley walked to West Peace River, to the barber shop. There, according to Fred Blair, Bradley told his story in a calm and collected manner, beginning with the words, "Well, I've done it."

"Done what? What did you do?"

"Well, I've shot him."

"Who?"

"Harold."

"Where did you shoot him?"

"In the Jack Pine Flats. I will give myself up to you if you will take me over to the police."

"Alright. But first give me the gun and ammunition."

They immediately crossed over to the town where Bradley gave himself up.

Edith Bradley, a witness at the preliminary hearing, told about her meeting and early relationship with Bradley, carrying her testimony forward in detail to the day of the shooting. What she said was not helpful to Bradley. It is significant that Charlie Roberts, who appeared for Bradley at the preliminary inquiry, made no objection to the girl's testimony, perhaps because those closely related to the proceedings felt the marriage was not valid. Certainly at the beginning of the criminal proceedings, Bradley needed all the help he could get.

Shocked by the killing, sympathy at first turned against Bradley, but as the trial date drew near, public opinion began to change. It is a fascinating study of how the residents of a closely knit small town may change their thinking in a short time. At first, mirroring the community's sentiments, the local paper referred to Harold Smith as a "well-known and popular young man." Even more damaging to Bradley was a direct quote. When asked if he had shot the father too, he replied, "No, I am glad I did not have to injure him, as it was not him I was after." Jean Kelley wrote that poor Harold was buried in an especially-made coffin to accommodate his six-foot, four-inch body.

The next edition had this to say about Edith Bradley at the preliminary inquiry: "She, considered the indirect cause of the shooting, expressed no sympathy for her husband." According to the paper, Bradley's only friend was Mrs. Cook, his wife's mother, who expressed the deepest sympathy for him – and probably paid for his legal expenses.

Chief prosecutor E.B.Cogswell, K.C.,arrived from Edmonton. He had a strong voice and could look very fierce when required to deal with an evasive witness. McKay, the defense counsel, was a big burly man. Colourful, emotional, with a commanding presence and a well-tuned voice, he had a grand way with a jury.

The evening before the trial, both my parents and we children were surprised and delighted when the Andersons arrived. Mother thanked her lucky stars that she had a large roast in the oven. John said they had found land with good soil near a couple they had known all their lives. It was about twenty-five miles from the Crossing, near the present-day town of Berwyn. They had planned a later trip for supplies, but after reading the account of the Bradley preliminary hearing decided to come earlier for the trial.

Dad, as usual, was up and off at six the following morning. The Andersons, who had again pitched their tent alongside of ours, were not far behind. Dad had warned them that they would have to stand in line if they hoped to get seats. Mother was happy to stay with the children. She had been horrified at the cold-blooded manner that Bradley had used to deal with Harold Smith.

There had to be strong leanings towards a murder conviction. Giving the highest value to Bradley's story, the amount of force he claimed he was threatened with – the buggy whip – did not justify the fire power with which he responded.

Except for Bradley entering the witness box to give evidence on his own behalf, the court followed pretty well the evidence given at the preliminary inquiry. There was, however, one major difference: the cross-examination of the Crown witnesses by McKay. Toward those whom he felt would look with sympathy upon Bradley, he took a soft approach. Only while questioning W.E. Smith, did McKay thunder and challenge his testimony.

There was a stir in the court when Ralph Bradley was put in

the witness box. He tearfully told of the happiness of himself and his wife until Harold Smith appeared on the scene, their gradual estrangement, and finally their separation, when she exclaimed, "Ralph, don't you dare touch me! I hate you, you've ruined my life!" In turn, Bradley was subjected to a powerful cross-examination by Cogswell. He had difficulty reconciling some of his statements and explaining certain of his actions, but he did not lose his composure.

During the final summing up, McKay gave a powerful and convincing address. He had much material to draw upon – the "wife stealing"; the accusation that the Smiths had so abused and threatened Bradley, he required a pistol to defend himself; that Bradley feared those big, powerful men, and seeing them dismount with the intent to batter and possibly kill him, shot in self-defence.

Scorning the middle course that asked for a verdict of manslaughter, McKay then stood tall before the jury and demanded a complete acquittal. By then, McKay was speaking to the already converted. Anything the Crown prosecutor had to say, fell on deaf ears. The judge directed the jury to either find the accused guilty or set him free.

Though she did not go to the trial, it was Mother who loved to tell the story that on the final day of Ralph Bradley's trial, a pall of dust hung over the town, and by noon the streets were lined with buggies, democrats, and saddle horses, as settlers for miles around came in to hear the verdict. By the time Dad finished his deliveries the theatre was packed, but he, along with others, was able to hear what was going on through the open door. The jury retired for only fifteen minutes before returning with the verdict, "Not guilty." Mother heard the cheering of the jubilant crowd from the movie theatre, where the trial was held, to their tent over a mile away.

Applause and wild cheering filled the air as spectators put Bradley on their shoulders and surged from the building to join the people waiting outside. Bradley was the man of the hour, the popular hero of the day. The celebrations spilled across the town and even into West Peace River.

Later that evening, my parents sat under the canopy with the Andersons. A full moon shed its eerie light on the valley as the four discussed the outcome of the case. John Anderson, a serious, thoughtful man, said that he felt T.A. Brick, the foreman of the jury, looked unhappy when he announced the not guilty verdict. He and my father agreed that there should have been a jail sentence and that the judge had overstepped his responsibility in siding with McKay's demand they either find the accused guilty or set him free.

The police were not happy with the verdict. Corporal Hatfield, who reported the proceedings, made this observation: "The verdict appeared to be very popular with certain classes." No doubt Bradley was not his idea of a popular civic hero. The last sentence of Hatfield's report stated, "Bradley with his wife and party left immediately after the trial for Nebraska, USA."

It is astonishing that Edith, who had privately and publicly said that Ralph Bradley had ruined her life, that she did not love him and wanted nothing more to do with him, went back to him. But she was young and impressionable. She had been an actor as well as a fascinated spectator throughout the proceedings. She had watched, wide-eyed, the dramatic end of the case when Bradley, declared by law to be not guilty of murder was set free, then taken up and made the man of the moment by a shouting, cheering mob. All these events had mesmerized her, made him a heroic figure, and pushed her back into his arms.

There are no records to show what took place in the lives of these two after they left the north. Did they remarry? Did they stay together? We have the chronicle of their first turbulent year together and then they disappear from the records.

CHAPTER SEVENTEEN

Over the Mighty Peace

D ad chose a beautiful day to show Mother the homestead, when the hills were bright with colour. Lowbush cranberries blazed brightest in scarlets and reds, while slender birch and aspen, growing close to the narrow trail, showed the mellower hues of yellows and oranges. Here and there, dark green clumps of jackpine contrasted with the summer-browned grass of the hills.

Climbing higher, they could see the river, its placid surface reflecting the vivid blue of the sky. Overhead, geese flying in V-formations, honked their goodbye to the dying season, reminding Mother that all-too-soon the land would be caught in the icy grip of winter. One perfect bright leaf drifted down onto her lap. Absently, Mother flicked it away and mentally began building her new house.

As the team climbed slowly over the hills, Dad had plenty of time to point out the other homesteads. Hastily-built shacks set among the hills had a deserted, lonely look. Dad said they likely belonged to bachelors or married men who lived in town, who spent only the minimum time there required to prove up the land. On the other hand, many men sent their wives and children to brave the rigours and loneliness of bush life, while they earned much-needed cash in town.

However, one shack looked very much lived in. Children and a dog played catch while a black and white cat watched from the top of a fence post. The Hees family lived there. Like many others, August Hees moved his butcher shop to Peace River when Grouard folded. After a few months, his wife and family moved to the hills to a small shack with a canvas top, while he ran his shop in town. That first year in Peace River had not been easy for Mrs. Hees. Like Mother, she had never lived on a farm before. She had to learn to milk cows, raise poultry, and care for her growing family. She was never lonely, though, as the road went right through their land and other farmers stopped to buy fresh meat from her husband. They made a good living off the farm. Now a large two-storeyed house was being built for them.

Mother would have to do her stint on the land too. But for now she was enjoying the countryside. At our homestead, she was delighted to find the odd, small meadow with little bluffs of trees here and there. Dad said they might yield enough wild hay to feed the horses for a winter. After our picnic lunch, I slept while Mother and Carlton helped Dad choose a site for the cabin he would build in the spring.

Just as they were leaving, they saw a huge moose standing by a rotted spruce – a shaggy-coated, tremendous creature, with racks maybe six-feet wide, covered with white fuzz. Mother said he looked magnificent. Dad nearly spoiled her day when he said with a wicked grin, "Don't get too carried away, that moose could feed us for an entire year." As if he understood, the huge animal, with a disdainful toss of his antlers, turned and walked slowly towards the forest. But Dad was only fooling. Although he never made an issue of it, I never knew him to kill a wild animal, although he may have shot an owl in order to save his chickens. A family of deer wandered the trails on our Shaftsbury farm for years.

• • •

It was the middle of December when Dad moved us into a wooden shack close to where our tent had been. The weather had turned very cold, with strong winds coming off the river threatening to lift the tent from its platform. With the baby expected in a few weeks, we needed a better space. The shack, hastily built, was without insulation except for tar paper on the inside. This made it look dark and gloomy, especially with a thick layer of frost covering the windows, but at least we could now move in some of our furniture.

Mother and Dad had been heating the tent with the cookstove, keeping a roaring fire going all day. At night, Dad banked it with green wood, a procedure that had to be repeated every few hours. It was grim, getting up in bitter cold weather. Mother said he never complained. We had a good wood stove but with temperatures around fifty below zero, it only warmed the air at a radius of a few feet. To give us some comfort, Dad wrapped heated boulders and put them at the foot of our beds. With sweaters over our nightgowns, we slept through the night, usually finding our blankets frozen to the wall in the morning. It must have been quite a task keeping Carlton and me off the icy floor with games we could play in bed. Mother often bundled us up and took us out. After a short while we were happy to come in, our little faces rosy and eyelashes white with frost. She was no longer deceived by the dry atmosphere and bright sunshine, knowing that tender faces can freeze without awareness.

I can not imagine how my mother kept her sanity during those long, cold, winter months ahead – cooped up, everything jammed in together, along with two active children and a new baby born in January. When the temperature dipped to thirty and forty below, we must have been confined to the bed, as the floor was freezing cold. The worst feature of the tent, according to Mother, was a dripping ceiling during sudden thaws.

I was too young to remember those first winters, but do remember, of later years, our farm kitchen on a winter morning – firewood stacked near the stove, a bucket for slops near the door, coffee perking on the back of the big range, my father shaving at the kitchen table, and I in my petticoat, washing my neck and arms at the corner washstand, while Mother stirred the porridge and eggs sputtered in the frying pan. Farm kitchens had to be functional, not beautiful. Ours was bathroom, dining room, laundry, and in the early days, the dairy. Each in turn and sometimes all at once. But we did have our bedrooms and the front room.

In the tent, however, we had been under Mother's feet all the time. She never mentioned it though, except to sympathize with her neighbours – a young English couple who were spending their first northern winter living in a tent.

On January 27, Wilbur Junior was born. When he was first shown his new son, Dad said, in a serious tone that belied the twinkle in his eye, "We'll have to hide him Ollie, or they're sure to intern him." Mother considered the baby's wide-set violet eyes, fair hair, and square face, and agreed that although he did not resemble her as much as Carlton did, he did seem to take after the Dutch-German side of her family. He weighed ten pounds, the biggest of us all. After going through a long hard delivery, Mother was understandably exhausted and needed to sleep.

As Dad made his way down Main Street that blustery January morning, he ran into Pierre Gauvreau who was returning from the drug store with a suspicious-looking package under his arm. When Dad told him that he had just seen his new son, born late last night, Pierre chuckled, saying, "It just came over the wire that January 27 is also the Kaiser's birthday. So let's drink to Peace River's newest citizen." They started with a toast "for a long life for John Wilbur Junior and a short one for the Kaiser." This led to many more. Arriving at the hospital the next day, Dad said with a bewildered look, "You know, Ollie, I must have been right out of my mind last night. I woke up at 2 A.M. nearly frozen. I'd clean forgot to bank the stove." Mother did not approve of drinking, and liquor had never been a problem, except on such occasions. He looked so miserable that, instead of scolding, she insisted that he go and get a good meal. "After several hours sleep," he reported later, "I had a wonderful meal at the Peace Hotel, of soup, salad, vegetables, meat, and dessert. All for the sum of forty cents."

My parents did not have an idle moment that winter. Besides working from 7 A.M. until 1 P.M. for Mr. George, Dad worked for the town, clearing trees and brush for new streets, while waiting for work to start on the bridge. As there was no let up in the weather, he often came home nearly frozen. "You need warmer clothing," Mother told Dad. He answered, "We will need all our cash for a down payment on H.A.'s cattle." She helped by making him hearty meals and in any other way she could think of.

Weekly washing had been enough of a task, but now with diapers to launder every day there was no time to take us for walks. Instead, she wrapped me in a quilt, put me in my sled and, as Junior slept, I watched while she and Carlton filled the tubs with snow. They sometimes had a snow fight, which sent me into gales of laughter. This not only amused us, but gave Dad a break from hauling water. In a few hours, Mother brought in the clothes, frozen stiff as boards. The frost removed some of the moisture and they finished drying on lines strung across the room, filling the room with a wonderful fresh outdoor fragrance.

Then it was spring. One day, an explosive crack and a loud rumble shattered the early morning stillness. Startled, I ran to my mother. She whispered as she tucked me in beside her that it was only the ice breaking up and lulled me back to sleep.

Break-up always caused great excitement. Half the town rushed to the riverbank to see who would win the ice pool. Dad, who had intended buying a ticket, said that the steady rain we had been having would likely take the river out. He was right. The mighty Peace, older than the dinosaurs, was breaking up.

In the many years I lived across from the junction of these rivers, the Peace and the Smoky, the ice has never gone out the same way twice. Usually the little Smoky is the first to go. Rivulets of melting snow, along with rain, rush down the steep canyons lifting the ice and taking both rivers out with a mighty roar.

We were allowed to play on the small sandbar where the creek ran into the Peace, but were warned to keep away from the river. With steep cliffs on this side it was swift, deep, and treacherous. Some years later, the Mighty Peace nearly claimed me for its own.

I was ten and a half and old enough to know my own mind. Dad warned us to take the long way home, behind the town and over the Peace Bridge, to avoid crossing the river itself. It was March and we had had a chinook that raised temperatures forty degrees in a short time. Torrents of water from snow melting on the hills ran into the river and caused the ice to crack.

It had been a day filled with excitement. We had stayed after school hoping for a part in the "Good Health" play directed by Susan Stewart. I was named to play the Sunshine Fairy. Mrs. Stewart said that I looked like sunshine, with my pretty yellow hair. I walked part of the way home with Mavis Murphy who had been chosen to play the Water Fairy. We were two fairies, walking on air, imagining the fantastic costumes to be made for us. She left me at the end of Main Street and I came down to earth again. I was alone now, and knew that I had to hurry if I was to cross the river and walk the two and a half-miles to our farm before dark. Walking quickly across the bridge that spanned the Heart River, I noticed that the ice was covered with water.

The ice road crossing the Peace seemed solid enough. I hesitated, thinking of Dad's warning. But to take the long way home meant an extra two and a half mile walk and the sun was sinking fast. Contemplating the dark woods along the trail and the eerie call of the coyotes from the hills above, I decided to ignore Dad's warning.

Turning right at the end of the bridge, I headed towards the river, passing the Indian children's burial ground. Facing the river was the Beulah Boat Company sign, where my friends learned to spell my name. Jagged cakes of ice flanked the ice road, although the road itself had been smoothed out early in the winter.

I was three-quarters of the way across the river when I saw a gap in the ice, cutting the road in half. I knew I should turn back but I followed to the right over the rough surface, to where I felt I could jump across. Carefully climbing over a jagged ice ridge, I looked down at the black water, and shivered. The shore was so close and the lights of my friend's house on the west side of the river were less than a quarter of a mile away, while behind me the town seemed a long way off. I took a cautious step towards the opening, sighing with relief when it held my weight. I was sure that I had jumped farther than this before. Bending my strong legs slightly, I sprang forward, and landed on the other side. My relief was short-lived. There was a loud crack, and the ice under me gave way.

As the frigid water encased me, I seemed to be standing apart, watching from several feet away, encouraging myself in the struggle to survive. In reality, I grabbed onto a jagged piece of ice and gave a mighty heave which enabled me to pull myself out. I had gone in up to my armpits. As the numbing cold penetrated my dripping clothes, I looked towards the house for help, feeling certain that I had seen someone at the window. No one appeared. Still gazing towards the house, smelling the pungent smoke from its fireplace, I became aware that my teeth had begun to chatter and I was trembling. I turned instead towards home. I tried to hurry, but my whole body was so numb with the cold that I could only plod along.

I warmed up a bit climbing the steep hill to the Shaftsbury Trail and thereafter made better time. I passed the one-room schoolhouse that had been closed since we moved to the St. Germain place. Another quarter of a mile and I climbed the long Deacon Hill. Stopping to rest at the top, I felt my knees to see what had been scratching them. I discovered that it was my dress, frozen solid and protruding through the gap in my coat.

It was nearly dark now, but my eyes had become accustomed to the fading light and I was able to make out the brooding outline of the jack pines that bordered the road to the left. The riverbank on its far side curved to make room for the little island below, while old Misery Mountain loomed up to the right like a warm comforting friend. I trudged down the hill, too exhausted to walk much farther, when I saw a shadowy figure coming towards me. I was startled and a bit frightened. Who would be walking down this trail at night?

"Is that you, Beulah?"

No music ever sounded as beautiful as my mother's voice that night. We stood in the dark – she felt my wet clothes. Then she cried out when she realized what must have happened. She took me in her arms and held me against her warm body, saying, "Dad wouldn't believe me! I came as soon as I could."

It was the only time she had ever come to meet any of us. She was usually too tired after helping Dad with the dairy, with cooking and caring for the seven of us to walk that far at the end of the day. Her intuition told her how great was my need. It was no longer necessary for me to be brave, and I sobbed as I told her what had happened.

"Should I have gone to Nettie's house?" They had not even a team and sleigh, nor an extra coat they could spare, anymore than we had.

Agreeing with my decision, she said, "You had enough confidence in yourself to make it the hard way." We had always been able to read each other's mind, and when she said, "Our great Father takes care of his own. If we ask he sends help to us," I believed her.

We were exhausted when we finally reached the hill below the house. Dad and Carlton had been worriedly watching for us and came down to help us up the hill.

Lying in my warm bed that night, I overheard my parents discussing how close they had come to losing me. My father's statement surprised me. "Beulah may not look it, but she's strong. She walks the four miles to and from school, and she lifts those heavy cases of milk bottles while helping you wash them." I never complained about my chores again. I have often wondered if he knew I was listening to that sage remark.

A year later, I had another frightening experience on the river. But this time both Carlton and Junior were with me. It was in March again, and another sudden chinook sent rivulets of melted snow down Misery Mountain to the river. With a foot of ice water on our road, our rubber boots that only came up to our ankles were not adequate. Realizing that we would need a ride to school, Dad was wondering how he was going to manage in his small milk wagon, when our new neighbour stopped and offered us a lift.

Dad hesitated, for this man was a new Canadian who might not understand that he would have to go around by the bridge. Dad told him he had just barely got through yesterday, and he did not want another accident. With his son interpreting for him, the man said that he understood. We were heaved up and on our way. But when he came to the top of the hill, our neighbour pointed to the river, saying, "O.K. O.K.," and started down the hill. Seeing only surface water on the ice, and not having heard Dad's warning, we did not worry until we were two hundred yards from the other side.

It all happened so quickly we could not believe that the horses were swimming. The man, sweat pouring down his face, began beating them and yelling at them in his own language as he tried to keep their heads above water. There was no time for panic. With fascination we watched the gallant team's struggle to keep from being swept down river. I wondered why we were along side the team, and then saw that the grain box, with all seven of us standing in it, had floated off the wagon and was attached only to the team by the reins in the man's hands. If one of us had made a move, the grain box would have tipped and we would have been dumped into the icy river. We were saved by the short distance and the fact that we had been upstream from the team. The screaming that we had been hearing was from our school friends, watching from the high bank above, who thought we were going to drown.

It was as Dad suspected. The little Heart River had gone out, taking a few yards of the Peace with it. I do not know how our new neighbour cleared himself with my father – who, himself was "in Dutch" with Mother. She had told him not to let us go with the newcomer.

We were heroes for a day with our teachers and friends, even though we had hardly had time to be frightened.

CHAPTER EIGHTEEN

Pioneer Projects

The site my parents chose to build their first home was a pretty one – on a knoll overlooking a small pond encircled with willows. We were to spend many happy hours there in the future, with Carlton poling us over that pond on the raft that Dad made for us. Behind it was a bluff of poplars where the pasture began. Although our site was set back a ways, it gave us a good view of the road that marched straight along the dividing fence between our place and the Tom Lynch quarter.

The day we moved had been a busy day for my parents. Dad and Mother had worked hard putting up the big tent that was now home to us. Mother worked on the mosquito nets that she had laboriously hand sewn and managed to fasten to the ceiling of the tent. My job was to watch Junior while mother cooked supper on the range under the awning.

The nice white netting surrounding my baby brother and me looked boring, so I poked all five fingers through it. Junior kicked his fat legs and gurgled his approval. I thought the holes looked nice and was busy making more when my mother looked in to see how we were doing.

"Beulah?" she asked in a frigid voice, "How did those holes happen to get into the netting?"

I was only three, but I knew that I was in trouble. I decided to take the coward's way out, and said, "I 'spect Junior did it."

Junior was only four months old. Mother had been raised by her Aunt Em who believed in absolute truthfulness. She decided then and there to instill a little of this in me. I was hauled outside but before I got my first lick, I let out such a howl that Carlton ran to my defense. I even frightened Junior, who started to cry. Dad and Ernie Raymond, our young neighbour to the south, coming in from cutting logs for our cabin, were alarmed by my loud cries and ran up the hill. It seems that my first spanking was only remembered by my mother.

We were having a special supper that evening as Ernie had brought liver from the Lawrences' where he helped butcher a pig early that morning. The Lawrences had settled on their land a few years before us and put up an ice house, hauling ice from the river and sawdust from McRae's Lumber Mill. Except for the odd chicken, we would not have fresh meat this summer, so the liver was greatly appreciated. Mother was also glad H.A. had included onions to send along with Dad, and a bag of other vegetables from his root cellar. They were just what she needed to go with the liver, mashed potatoes, biscuits, and the custard from the seven eggs her twelve hens had presented her with that day.

After dinner, as everyone sat near the range under the awning, Dad got started on his African adventure stories. Suddenly, a big barn owl settled on a tree near the chicken coop. Ernie, who was a great tease, decided to take some of the wind out of Dad's sails by betting that he could not hit the owl. Actually, an owl's body is very small, only the feathers make it look large. Dad knew it would take a good shot to get him from this distance in the fading light.

Dad was confident as he rushed into the tent and got his .22 rifle. He fired and the owl fell to the foot of the tree. Dad heaved a sigh of relief, thinking that he had at last shut Ernie up. Not for long though. Mother decided she needed the feathers for a pillow – so Dad and Ernie plucked the owl. The bird had not a mark on it. He had not hit it at all! After puzzling over this, Ernie said that the owl must have been listening to Dad's great hunting exploits, and when he was shot at, he simply died of fright.

Dad and Ernie soon had the logs for the cabin peeled and stacked to dry. As Ernie would be leaving soon, Dad decided that they would fence the pasture before tackling Mother's garden. For the time being the horses were content to graze nearby, but he would be in a bad way if they decided to wander off. Besides, we had no plow.

When Carlton told Mr. Lothrope that Dad needed a walking plow, he drove to the Holt homestead to get the one they had borrowed from him and no longer needed and brought it over. Dad was grateful, and asked him in for a cup of coffee and Mother's freshly baked bread. As the tantalizing scent floated towards them, the older man was happy to accept. For lack of butter, Mother used globs of thick cream skimmed from the pans of milk she had let set overnight. When sprinkled generously with sugar and cinnamon, it tasted delicious. She also made a hit with her doughnuts. These were pieces cut from a loaf of risen dough, fried in hot fat to a golden brown, then dipped in the cinnamon-sugar mixture.

Although Dad had not forgotten how to milk a cow, he had never done much plowing on his father's farm, but Tom Lynch, our neighbour to the east, soon had him plowing fairly straight furrows. Carlton and Mother helped, and even I was allowed to drop the potato eyes into the holes Dad had made. Mother's garden was soon planted.

Dad needed no instructions for clearing the land – just his strong back and good right arm. Sharpening his axe, he went to work. Except for a grove of spruce to the north, his quarter was sparsely wooded. But even so, unexpected help was welcome. After nursing and bathing Junior, Mother put him down for his morning nap, telling Carlton and me to look after him. Then she donned her sun bonnet, her old moosehide gloves, and pulled Dad's old overalls over her skirt, ready to help on the land.

Crossing the meadow, she was deeply aware that the whole country was very quiet and open and free. This was why everyone they met was in such good spirits – like the country, their outlook had a fresh quality.

Mother surprised Dad with the amount of clearing she accomplished as she slowly and steadily hacked away at the underbrush and small trees with her sharp hatchet. She always preferred outside chores to housework and was enjoying herself. The air was like wine, the skies blue, and the sunshine would be with them until ten o'clock at night. When her arms and back tired, she switched to piling brush. Her favourite job, as it had a bit of excitement to it, was taking the reins and urging the team on, while Dad pried out the stumps with his crowbar. It was not long before a small field emerged, giving them a great sense of accomplishment.

Dad did not have a rake, so he made a stone boat of logs fastened together to drag over the broken sod and level the ground. Then he hand-seeded the field with oats, knowing that if the crop did not ripen, he could use it for green feed. He managed to cover the seed by fastening large clumps of willows to a bar that he attached to the whipple trees and dragged across the field. This was how Frank Mearon and his nephew Sid Brown had managed to harvest the first crop in the district of High Prairie, according to Sid.

Dad had only just finished sowing when ominous black clouds loomed on the horizon. He swiftly unharnessed the team and pastured them before the full fury of the storm broke, splitting the clouds asunder. A deluge of rain spilled down, soaking him to the skin. We stood under the tarp beside Mother, who was holding Junior, and laughed as we watched him run for the tent. It was a good thing he did run. Seconds after he passed under a big poplar, it was hit by a bolt of lightning. The bolt passed so close that it knocked Dad to the ground. He reached us, white and shaken, and we clung to him, thankful that only the tree was shattered.

That same tree near the pasture became my summer playhouse. I sat on its fallen trunk for hours with my family of twig dolls. It took a bit of searching to find branches with a V in the right place for their limbs. But dressing them was easy – with leaves for their dresses, a crocus for a spring hat, a wild rose for a summer one, and a bright red rose-hip for the fall.

My fondest memories of the homestead are those golden summer days spent poling our little raft on our shallow pond.

We sat for hours watching schools of tadpoles swimming among the bullrushes. Mother explained they were the babies of the bull-frogs that lulled us to sleep, and we were careful not to harm them, nor the fascinating daddy-long-legs walking on the water.

One day Mother found me sitting by the pond, talking, she thought, to myself. As she came closer, it seemed that it was to my companions – a family of ladybugs I was carefully holding in my apron. "Throw those nasty bugs away, Beulah," she said in a stern voice. "It isn't nice to play with insects." I stared at her, my brown eyes full of concern.

"But I likes them," I said, and carefully coaxed one onto my finger, holding it up for her to admire.

Our life overflowed with activities. I slipped out at dawn with my father to watch the day awaken. As I ran after him, timid eyes seemed to be following me. One day we found a meadowlark's nest hidden in the tall grass. It was filled with fledglings whose wide-open yellow beaks seemed to dwarf their small naked bodies. Another time I saw a nervous, furry field mouse scurry between the stalks of grain.

Dad made a play pen for Junior from small poles, with a piece of canvas for shade and Mother's quilt beneath it which he placed on the stone boat. There Junior could play and sleep wherever they were working.

One day we were in the field when we heard a familiar sound. It was Brownie's excited bark as she came tearing across the field. She had been left with the Andersons when we moved. We were glad to have her back, and to welcome the Andersons who were not far behind. They had been in town before Christmas, a month before Junior was born, and had offered to keep her until spring. They decided now that their crop was in and the boys out of school, it was a good time to return Brownie and help Dad with his buildings.

Work stopped for the day. Mother said later it was like a three-ringed circus with everyone talking at the same time. Edith was amazed when she saw Junior who was big for his age. But when we tried to get him to show off, he whimpered for his mother. I was angry when they all laughed at Dad's remark, "He's bushed like the rest of us."

The Andersons had stopped at H.A. George's farm for directions, and the good man sent along a sack of vegetables and a big parcel of meat, saying that he owed Mother a favour. It was true enough. Shortly after Dad started working for him, he had persuaded her to care for his sick child, Emma, who was my age. Knowing that he had had more than his share of grief, having lost his wife and baby daughter a little over a year before and his eldest son at an earlier date, she had not the heart to refuse, although it meant leaving us with a neighbour. She stayed until one day, while rocking Emma in a reverie, she glanced down and was shocked to see Emma's dark little head instead of my fair one, and she wondered what she was doing there when her own little ones needed her. Mr. George solved his problem by marrying Jeanette McEwan, the matron of the new Peace River hospital.

The Andersons soon had their tent up. While the women prepared lunch, Dad and John went over their plans. They would not need many tools, John said. Just a hammer, an axe, and a saw. He nodded with approval when he saw that Dad's axe was as sharp as his own. It had to be, in order to make a good job dovetailing the logs. Gordon and Allen Anderson, stripped to their waists, were soon poling around the pond with Carlton and me. They soon built their own raft from a couple of Dad's peeled logs tied together.

We were up bright and early the next morning. While Dad and John attended the chores, Carlton and the boys took Mr. Lothrope his milk, along with a request for a shovel. The women helped too, working like a relay team, scooping up buckets of soil and dumping them onto the stone boat. They were glad the basement was to be small. Several feet of dirt had to be left along the edge to carry the weight of the logs, as they had no cement.

Having just learned the art of dovetailing, John was glad when Mr. Lothrope dropped by to give his opinion. When he saw that they were doing a good job he left for town, taking mother's grocery list. Along the way, he stopped to talk to neighbours, mentioning that Dad could use some help in order to get his buildings up before winter. He made it back in time for supper and afterwards we all sang to the accompaniment of his harmonica. As Mr. Lothrope was leaving he said, looking a trifle smug, "I have a hunch that your cabin will be up before you know it."

He was right. During the next couple of weeks, hardly a day passed without a neighbour riding over, his tools strapped to his saddle, ready to lend a hand. Johnnie Lawrence was the first to put in a couple of days. Next to appear was Cephas Northey, and after that Tom Lynch. To my parents' gratitude, a good-sized cabin of neatly dovetailed logs was raised. It still needed a roof, doors, and windows, but the difficult part was finished.

Soon Dad and John were off for lumber to finish the house. Although George McRae now owned the mill, it was situated on Floyd Gilliland's homestead, about two and a half miles north of us in a thick forest of virgin spruce. The first place they passed was that of W.E. Smith, a carpenter and cabinet maker by trade. Smith may have owned the sawmill prior to McRae, as their land bordered Gilliland's and during the Bradley trial their place was referred to as "The Mill."

Shortly after the tragic death of their son, Harold, Mr. Smith started a sash and door factory in town, turning his farm over to their daughter Beulah Aikens and her husband Clarence. It must have taken considerable courage for the Smiths to remain in the district after the damaging remarks of the judge and the lawyer for the defense. However, my parents were to learn that most people who knew the Smiths thought the judge and jury had made a great mistake.

At the sawmill, both wagons were soon loaded with the flooring and material for the roof. The windows, doors, stove pipe, and other details would have to wait until Dad's next trip to town. The house, when finished, measured thirty by twenty-four feet. It was to be divided into a living room, three bedrooms, and a kitchen. A lean-to kitchen was added later. John's help had been invaluable. As he said, having recently built his own cabin with his friends' help, it was a cinch.

Dad then outlined his plan for a makeshift barn. The walls would consist of two rows of posts set in the ground about three feet apart. To these he would attach chicken wire to hold the straw that he would tamp in between for insulation. A couple of neighbours had agreed to let him have the straw for next to nothing after they thrashed. He would probably need the straw, in any event, as a supplement for spring feeding. He was to take delivery of his cows from H. A. George during the summer, giving him time to build a log barn before winter.

For Mother, these friends had not come too soon. Dad had been around the neighbourhood and had an occasional trip to town, but with three children to care for while keeping house in a tent, Mother had not spoken with another woman for over two months.

The Andersons left after the cabin roof was on, promising, if all went well, to visit for a week-end in the fall. My parents had no words to express their gratitude. Just a hug and a handshake. The shining eyes of their friends spoke more plainly than words – in sharing their toil they had also shared their pleasure, days of work, and evenings of laughter and song.

Dad finished the flooring of tongue-grooved quarter-inch planks cut the right length. It was easy to fit and nail in place. Mr. Lothrope came over and helped with the doors and windows. The day finally came when Dad brought out our furniture, in storage for over a year.

Mother's wedding gifts were the first to be unpacked. The most prized was a cut-glass bowl of heavy leaded crystal, a gift from her Aunt Em. We were not supposed to touch it, but we sometimes watched a sunbeam as it caught a point of crystal, setting it afire with brilliant colours. Another possession we children loved was a cupid carved from wood, holding a large red heart. Mother said it was a memento from a young man she nearly married. Then there was my father's silver cigarette box. Although he hardly gave it a glance, Mother and we children loved it. Engraved with the Queen's initials, it had been presented to him for outstanding service during the Boer War.

I remember best Mother's rocking chair and the big rug she was anxious to put down. It would protect Junior's knees now that he was learning to crawl. Chintz drapes from the hotel were strung on wires across the interior and served as room partitions during the first year in the new house. It was not until Dad brought in the trunks of clothes that Mother wished they had brought just one of the many chests of drawers left behind in Grouard. But she had brooded enough. She found pleasure in their neat cabin, fragrant with the clean odor of new wood and bright with sunshine.

Dad helped her move in the orange crates they had been using for cupboards. They were not very practical now that the baby was crawling, but then Mother recalled she had never had a cupboard that would keep out a small child. She laughed, remembering the orange crate idea had come from an Indian stopping house. "And now we're in the same boat."

Waylaying the Aikens on their way to town, Mother asked Beulah Aikens to buy two packages of dye with thread to match. Seeing what Mother was up to, Beulah offered the loan of her treadle sewing machine. After the first lesson, there was no holding Mother. From her stock of white sheets she produced window curtains, a cover for the single bed that served as a couch, and several cushions. She dyed them all a deep forest green and trimmed them with the same flowered chintz she had used for the substitute partitions.

We were no sooner settled in when the Lawrence family dropped by to inspect Dad's straw barn and our new cabin. When they saw Mother's handiwork made from the sheets and drapes Dad had wanted to leave behind, they were impressed. Johnnie said with a laugh, "You're not doing badly for a couple of greenhorns."

They had also come to invite us to a berry-picking picnic in the hills above the river brakes. A bachelor friend, who had a homestead there, had just shot a young bear and offered to cook them bear steaks. Mother wanted to back out, but seeing the look of anticipation in Dad's brown eyes, changed her mind and offered to bring a German potato salad, saying the recipe had been in the family for generations. Dad sighed with relief, but said, "I hope this won't get us all interned."

The berry-picking picnic was a real event for us. I can still close my eyes and see the bachelor's little cabin perched on the ledge above the river. Mother followed Mrs. Lawrence and the girls into the cabin with the baby, while Carlton and I went around the corner where the men were examining the thick black bear hide draped over a log. Its head and feet still were intact; its glassy eyes stared. Carlton and I were both shaken at the sight, and he only shook his head when I asked him why it did not run away.

Although my parents were enjoying their bear steak, Carlton and I and the Lawrence girls preferred their mother's fried chicken. By the time we finished off the rhubarb pie and the cake, we had completely forgotten the poor bear.

When my parents went out to pick berries, Mother persuaded me to stay with Junior, saying he might be shy for he did not know Cosie Lawrence who was to baby-sit. Dad was the first to return with his pail brimming over with big juicy saskatoons. According to Mother, Dad always found the best patches in trees six- to eight-feet high loaded with big juicy berries hanging like grapes. It was then, she said, that his mischievous nature got the better of him. After grabbing off the biggest bunches he moved on again, always staying out of sight until he had his bucket full. Mother was very indignant when she straggled back with the others only to find him asleep in the democrat.

CHAPTER NINETEEN

Lights and Highlights

Summer's long sunny days began to shorten with the approach of fall. Dad finished swathing and Mother, with our help, gathered in the vegetables. Soon the darkness of the northern winter would close in.

When the call went out for men to help build the new bridge across the river, Dad signed on, always glad to earn extra cash. But the work in the bitter cold was hard, and it meant rising long before first light to feed and water the stock. Our only water supply was a creek about a mile up the road, and it had to be chopped free of ice each morning. Mother's breakfast of porridge, bacon, eggs, and coffee was ready when he returned from the chores. Always an optimist, Dad left with a smile and a reassurance that things would be better in the spring. Mother was beginning to appreciate why they called this "next year country." However, she took pleasure in viewing her jars of preserves lining the new shelves. Besides the berry-picking outing down to the brakes last summer for saskatoons, there had been others for blueberries and lowbush cranberries. Wild blueberries were my favourite. When I had the flu and refused to eat, Mother could always coax me with eggnogs flavored with her special blueberry preserves.

One night Dad returned home with a small package containing a small piece of salt pork, worth only a few cents, that he had picked up on the road. "I wonder who the poor devil was who lost this?" he said. Although only five at the time, I've never forgotten his compassion for someone worse off than himself.

For our family the most important event of 1917 was the birth of my brother, Warren, on a cold December night. He distinguished himself by arriving in the sleigh on the way to the hospital. Dad, trying to hurry the team over the rough, icy road nearly panicked when he heard the baby's first plaintive cry. Although he had tucked Mother in the back of the sleigh and covered her with warm quilts, Mother could still feel the baby's tiny body tremble from the cold. At the hospital, she told the nurses that she was fine, but asked them to hurry and get the baby in out of the cold, as his teeth were chattering. The next day she asked why they had all laughed. The nurse replied that a child born in a sleigh in such frigid weather was enough of a shock – but one with teeth that chattered was hilarious.

I told Mother I wanted this baby, because like me, he had brown eyes. She agreed, as long as I changed his diapers. I quickly decided I was too young, but perhaps I could manage the chore next year when I was five.

Dad was proud of his growing family and called us "the mob." According to Mother, he teased her by ticking off our names and counting us before leaving.

A cold wave ushered in the year 1918, with temperatures falling to minus fifty. But diapers still had to be washed, so Carlton and I were given the job of filling washtubs with snow. Mother learned early that water was never thrown out until it was thoroughly used – first for baths and personal washing, then for clothes and finally for scrubbing floors. After we were bundled up, only our eyes showing, we ventured out. In a short while our lips became stiff and we could not talk. The air lost so much moisture that we were thirsty most of the time. Yet, this extreme weather seemed to generate a certain excitement, as if the very elements of the universe were challenging us.

As a rule, these cold spells did not last long. The well-known chinook arch was not always visible this far north, but when cloudbanks appeared in the south-west, dry warm chinook winds soon spread across the country, causing temperatures to rise as much as fifty degrees in a short while.

In winter, the moon was the rightful queen of the heavens. When there was no wind and a bright crescent moon shone down, every twig, every bush that pushed up through the whiteness, stood out in the pale moonlight. We got up by moonlight and went to bed by moonlight, and a few years later, started off to school with the moon following behind us. It was at least ten in the morning before the sun climbed above Grouard Hill, only to disappear again by three in the afternoon.

Dad was now milking nine cows and delivering cans of milk to restaurants and the hospital. Sundays, when there was no delivery, he still had to haul our drinking water from the creek, and saw and split a week's supply of wood. It was exhausting work, but he figured he could afford to hire a man in the spring.

Occasionally, Dad took Mother to a Saturday night dance at Strong Creek. At first, dances were held in one of the larger homes and later in the Stewart School. When the Strong Creek Hall was built, deep shelves were placed along the wall behind the stage where babies and small children slept. Mother tucked us in and soon my brothers were asleep. However, I always stayed awake to watch the fun, and next day wound up the gramophone and taught my brothers to dance. It did not make a bit of difference whether the music was by Harry Lauder or a symphony, we danced merrily on while Mother rocked the baby to sleep.

The Aikens farm was only a mile from us. One day when her husband was away, Beulah Aikens asked Mother if I could spend the night. I was a shy child, and Mother was surprised when I agreed. Perhaps it was sharing our names that made us kindred spirits from the start. After that, whenever I was missing Mother knew exactly where to find me. Even a spanking, a rare occurrence in our family, did not stop me from visiting Beulah.

I'll never forget the sunny day Clarence Aikens rode over to invite Mother and me to tea. Mother frowned, "Oh, pshaw! Why did it have to be today?" It was my fifth birthday, an occasion not to be taken lightly. But we had had our baths and Mother had finished icing my cake, so she guessed she could spare a couple of hours. I would have to go in my everyday dress though; everything that I had not outgrown was in the wash.

I remember feeling very special as I skipped along the familiar trail beside Mother. But I was soon in trouble, with only myself to blame. Mrs. Aikens, entering with refreshments, heard me being scolded for chasing the cat. Embarrassed, I burst into tears. She offered to wash my tear-stained face, but first led me to her bedroom. There, laid out on her bed, was a beautiful pink dress that fitted me perfectly. I felt like a princess when she dressed me in it. After washing my face and brushing my blonde curls, she tilted the mirror so that I could see myself. I remember it as if it were yesterday.

• • •

Our parents were not happy when they learned that the school was to be held in Floyd Gilliland's home. It meant a three-mile walk each morning and afternoon. To us, the trail leading through the woods seemed incredibly long, with its corduroy and mudholes. The trip took about an hour and a half – allowing for a bit of dallying. There were other perils too.

One morning we stopped to pick berries when a man appeared and asked if we had seen a black horse. Carlton said, "No, but we heard noises coming from that bush over there." He told us to get along to school and looked as if he meant it, so we did. He dropped in on his way home, and introducing himself as Ed Holt, told my parents that after sending us along, he had seen a bear with her cubs in a patch not far from where we were picking berries. Mother was upset but, as Dad said, we could just as easily have met up with a bear on our own land.

Early one fall day, our teacher, Mrs. Currie, let Carlton and me out, warning us to go straight home as she could see smoke rising from the direction of our land. We were halfway home when smoke rose in a thick pall from the trail just ahead. A small fire smoldering in the muskeg near the trail had flared up and created the dense smoke. Heavy timber on either side was almost impassable, but Carlton said we would have to detour. After all, we had been told to go home. Grabbing my hand, he pulled me into the dense woods. When we finally emerged we were so exhausted we fell to the ground, happy to find that we were only a mile from home.

Our neighbour Tom Lynch found us, covered with scratches and mosquito bites, our clothes torn and dirty. Piggybacking me and half-carrying Carlton, he got us home. Tom told my parents that finding one's way through the timber would have been quite a feat for an adult, let alone an eight-year-old boy. My parents were thoroughly shaken, especially my mother, who knew the terrible fear of being lost. I was old enough to have doubts and fears, but with a child's faith never doubted Carlton's ability to get us through.

Mother and Dad were pleased when Duncan Stewart donated a corner of his land for a school, to be called the Stewart School. (For a long while our district of "84" was also known as the Stewart District, but is now called Weberville.) It would be ready in the spring of 1919. We would still have a three-mile walk but we would be a year older, and the trail passed through the farms of our friends and neighbours. Our new teacher, Jean Roy, was pretty but had an Irish temper. Although she often frightened me, I did learn to read and write.

When Mother found out that I spent most of my time at school playing with my best friend Elsie, she decided to keep me home. She needed my help now that Dad was selling eggs, especially with her ornery hens nesting in the bushes instead of the hen house Dad had built. Anyway, school would soon be closed for the winter. She also needed me to help with my little brothers. She was expecting her fifth child soon and the boys were a handful, especially Warren who, at a year and a half, was into everything.

Grandma had promised to be on hand for the event. but the stork arrived first. Late one frosty November night, Mother woke Carlton and me up. "Dad has to drive me to town," she said briskly, "and he might not be back until morning. I'm counting on you both to look after things until he gets back. Carlton, you'll have to stoke the fire, and Beulah, dress the little ones and keep them in bed till the house warms up. Carlton, help your sister cook the breakfast porridge."

I was only six at the time and my brother eight, yet Mother was confident that we would be able to look after ourselves and our two younger brothers until Dad returned.

As we watched from the window as Dad helped Mother into the sleigh, Carlton shook his head wisely and said, "She's gone to get us a new baby."

When Dad returned in the morning, smiling, he told us we had a new little sister. Marjory Katherine was born November 13, 1919. The first, and only, brunette in the family, she weighed seven pounds – small compared to my nine-pound birth weight.

My parents' situation had improved too. For the last two years, Dad had hired a neighbour with a breaking plow to work the land, and now it was paying off. Besides his crop of oats for green feed, he had forty acres of hard wheat ready to thrash.

It was exciting to watch the teams arrive, pulling racks loaded high with sheaves of grain. I envied Carlton, now eight, who with his short-handled pitchfork was helping Dad throw the sheaves onto the belt to be conveyed into the machine. It was fun to watch the grain pour from the long spout of the thrashing machine into the grain box on top of the wagon. The yield, around fifty bushels to the acre, was more than Dad had expected, and his small granary would not come close to holding it. Finally, he took Mother's suggestion and cleared out a small bedroom, shovelling the grain through the open window.

After the thrashers left, Carlton and I started filling sacks with wheat. What started out as fun became hard work, and before long we called to Dad to help us down. It was then that we heard a loud crack and felt the floor sink slightly. My parents heard it too and, while Mother pulled us out, Dad hurried for his team to haul in leftover logs to brace the floor.

It was a tough job – sawing the logs the right length, wrestling them down the cellar steps, then wedging them under the sagging floor – all by the light of a coal oil lamp. When

Mother tried to help him, Dad angrily shouted up the steps, "For God's sake, Ollie, stay with the kids. If the floor caves in, it will be bad enough with me down here." It seemed to take forever before he finally emerged, all smiles, saying as he put down his crowbar and sledge hammer, "I'm not sure how, but I managed it."

My parents were happy that night. The land had yielded a good harvest, and we had made it through another crisis. We had no need of the gramophone. Dad sang for us, as he had not for a long time, while we sat around the oil-drum heater.

I had run my legs off that day, helping Mother. I also looked after our latest baby, Marjory. I'll never forget that long evening, trying to keep her quiet while Mother fed the men. Jiggling her did not help. She was hungry. As I tried to comfort her, she latched onto my none-too-clean fingers, and when I tried removing them let out a piercing cry. Mother found me kneeling by her cradle, half asleep, the baby still sucking my fingers. She exclaimed, but as Dad carried me off to bed, he laughed, "You did ask Beulah to keep her quiet."

My darling little brother Warren was nearly two when Marjory was born. He was a tow-head with big brown eyes and, like me, walked when ten months old and was into everything. He did not know what to make of this new baby, who took up all his mother's time. And now even his Beulah was too busy to play with him. Warren was small for his age, but when fully grown was a little taller than his brothers.

In this land of the midnight sun, the season's first killing frost was often preceded by a display of northern lights. Entranced, we gazed upwards as the feathery bands of green, rose, and gold shimmered and danced across the sky. But this grand display did not lessen my parents' pain when they awoke the next morning to find their wheat crop frozen – good only for fodder – and the garden blackened and wilted except for the root vegetables. If it had not been for Dad's dairy and Mother's eggs, we would have been in a bad way.

The unpredictable climate convinced Dad that mixed farming was the only way, and he ordered two young Berkshire hogs from the United States. This superior breed, originally imported from Berkshire, England, were of a medium size with short legs, broad backs, and square hams. After winning first prize at the Peace River Agriculture Fair, Dad started getting orders for his sow's unborn litter.

I will never forget the fun and excitement of the fair. Dad drove us there in the democrat, while the hired man followed behind with Mother's leghorn chickens and Dad's pigs. We especially loved the horse races. Dad had told us that families had been arriving all week with their race horses. One outfit, believed to be the descendants of a tribe of Beaver Indians from just north of Fort St. John, had used the flat land along the river for the first racetrack in the country. Dad said these superb riders usually left with their share of the prize money.

We arived just in time to watch the first race. The air was thick with dust as the high-strung horses and their riders pranced and trotted their way down the river road towards the racetrack. Then the excited animals were manoeuvered into starting position and they were off, riding like the wind toward the finish line.

By the time Carlton and I were ten and eight, we were entering our cakes in the juvenile class and winning first and second prizes. After I was beaten by my brother two consecutive years, Mother confronted the judge and asked why her son's cakes won over her daughter's. It was the way we mixed the batter, the lady explained. Carlton stirred his, while I used a beating motion that caused bubbles. Years later, Mother reminded me of the morning she awoke smelling freshly baked cake and thought she was dreaming. In the kitchen, Junior and Warren watched with anticipation as Carlton and I lifted tiny cakes, baked in tin lids, from the oven. She was amazed at how good they tasted, and wondered how we had managed with spoons instead of measuring cups, as well as finding the right ingredients. But then, she said with a laugh, "You were always underfoot while I was baking." From then on, Mother let us help with the baking.

After the judging and races, Dad napped in the back of the

democrat with the two youngest, while Mother got the rest of us ready for the foot races. Our favourites were the three-legged and the sack races. We always got together with our neighbours for a picnic lunch. Then, after collecting our prize money, we piled into our democrat and headed contentedly home.

Other popular local get-togethers were dances. Before the Strong Creek Hall was built, dances were held in local homes, usually to the tune of a fiddle. One of the best fiddlers, according to Harry Clarke who often hosted these dances, was a Cree, Moshum St. Germain. My parents had seldom taken part in these early shindigs. Unlike the others, they could never sleep in, for the cows had to be milked and deliveries made. And Mother, always up early getting the five of us and our big meals ready, had by evening been glad to call it a day.

There was always a period in early winter before freeze up, when the ferries could not cross the river. But Dad had the responsibility of milk deliveries each day, so, like the few emergency cases, he was forced to cross over the partially constructed bridge. It was a bad experience. The bridge was narrow with no guard rails. The eighteen-hundred-foot structure was decked only with flat boards, about four inches wide and placed two inches apart, giving Dad and his team a view of the ice floes churning and grinding below. If Kate, who had only recently been broken to harness, should shy or jump, nothing could save the rig from going over. But they always made it safely across with Dad, on foot, leading the team. He was glad when the river froze over and he could cross on the ice.

Although there was little money, my parents always made Christmas an enchanting time for us. Preparations started early and Mother, a natural storyteller, entertained us as we helped with the baking and other chores. Dad, as sentimental about Christmas as Mother, always had time for that special shopping trip to town.

I still remember a shopping expedition to J.D. Levesque's Blue Store the year I was four. The little store was crammed with merchandise; toys even hung from the ceiling. Dad, wanting to show me off to the other shoppers, held me aloft to point out the doll carriage I wanted from Santa. It annoyed Mother. She thought how disappointed I would be Christmas morning when the carriage my parents could not afford was not under the tree. However, I was just as pleased with the doll's bed Dad had made me three Christmases ago when I was one. It always disappeared a few weeks before the big day, to reappear under the tree on Christmas morning with a fresh coat of paint and new bedclothes. And we always received something special from Grandma, who made sure her parcel arrived on time.

We always helped Dad choose the Christmas tree, tramping through the woods till we found just the right one. He waited until we were asleep Christmas Eve before bringing it in. It must have taken my parents half the night to decorate it. Early on Christmas morning, as soon as Dad had the house warmed up, he opened the door of our bedroom, and there it was – our beautiful tree, blazing with light from many candles reflecting off the wonderful ornaments Mother had been collecting since she was a child. At that time, before the town had electricity, we had not been spoiled by today's Christmas dazzle. The sight of the tree was pure magic for little children.

CHAPTER TWENTY

Reunions

Every two or three years, my grandmother, accompanied by our cousin Edward, visited for an indefinite period of time. They usually came in the spring. Her arrival seemed like Christmas all over again to us children, because she always brought gifts. Unlike Mother, who was happiest when working outside in her garden, Grandma enjoyed housework and baking.

I remember those times when, thinking Mother had hurt my feelings unnecessarily, she drew me into a little conspiracy. While the rest were out, we had a little tea party. It was also a lesson in etiquette about which she need not have bothered. Mother's training by Aunt Em in social graces had been even more rigid than hers. However, I loved the attention even more than the tea and goodies. She loved us all, but I was her favourite.

The visit I remember most vividly occurred just before my seventh birthday. It was a very special summer, for that was the summer that Grandmother and Edward, and Mother's sister, Aunt Eve, and her husband, Carl, visited us. The night before my Aunt Eve and her husband arrived at our homestead, Dad had cooped up a fat rooster for dinner, but in the rush to deliver his cans of milk and cream, forgot to chop off the bird's head. It would be a chickenless dinner unless Mother and Grandmother did the deed themselves. I was a coward and hid in the woodshed when I realized what was about to take place, until my curiosity got the better of me and I peeked through the cracks. I had to laugh in spite of the poor rooster's squawks. It really was a funny sight, my little grandmother endeavouring to hold the struggling bird's head over the chopping block, while trying to keep as far away as possible from the sharp axe my mother was brandishing. Grandma would have dropped the bird altogether if she had known that Mother turned her head away and shut her eyes before she swung the axe. The rooster gave another loud squawk, but he might have crowed. Mother had only managed to cut off the end of his beak. Grandmother put him back in the coop, relieved when Mother refused to try again. Mr. Lothrope saved the day when he stopped by for his milk and finished the bird off for them.

There was a twinkle, and an understanding look, in Dad's eyes that evening when I refused my share of the feast. I had slipped out while he was unharnessing the team and filled him in on the day's happenings. He surmised something of the sort when he was given a cool reception by Mother. He knew he had left his women in a bad situation, and was relieved when he was able to catch Mother's eye, with that hang-dog look that never failed, and was rewarded with a smile.

It was a wonderful evening. We children played while the grown-ups talked. Then we cuddled up close around the bonfire and listened as Dad's tenor harmonized with the professionals' in song, while the stars glistened and the trees whispered to the night.

My aunt and uncle had a vaudeville show. Their tour had taken them into the smaller cities and towns of western United States and Canada, with a fair amount of success. When the troupe visited Peace River, the whole town turned out, as well as many from the country. The hit of the evening was a musical impersonation of the comic characters Maggie and Jiggs. Aunt Eve played Maggie anad Uncle Carl was Jiggs. She had a beautiful soprano voice, and was so gifted and vivacious that she made quite a hit in our town, which had more than its share of talent. We were proud of her and enjoyed every moment as we basked in her reflected glory.

A few days later, the locals entertained the professionals with an impromptu show. Mrs. Stewart led off with her lovely contralto voice, followed by little Jimmy Connell, a happy-go-lucky Irishman with a magnificent tenor voice. Mrs. Ethel Steele, newly arrived from England, had been a music hall dancer and singer. She was very attractive and a natural for the leading roles in our local musical production, "Ben Hur and Esther." Her husband, Jimmy, was an outstanding ballroom dancer, as well as a proficient tap-dancer. He worked for the liquor board, but in his spare time passed on his skill to the local swains, while Ethel's Sunshine Girls were the pride of the town.

Another event the visitors greatly enjoyed was the Strong Creek sports day. We were up bright and early that day, with Dad promising to be back in time to make the ice cream. We anticipated a great day. The main attraction was baseball. The Holt brothers, plus Harry Clarke and a few neighbours, had set up a ball diamond and formed a team that was hard to beat. Horseshoes was another popular sport. In theory it was simple, but throwing a "ringer" from a distance, so a horseshoe encircled an upright iron rod, is not easy. With Dad and Uncle Carl, and my pretty aunt being coached by the local bachelors, it was a hilarious event.

The sports days were held after the crops were in. Many families had come to enjoy this annual outing, some from as far away as Bluesky. The sports events and community picnic brought a great deal of pleasure to all. But the main attraction for these early settlers was the chance to get together, and talk about world affairs, crops, and local conditions. It was also a time to meet newcomers.

Many of our neighbours were recent arrivals from other countries. The Watsons, who had settled near the banks of Strong Creek, were from Glasgow, Scotland. Another Scot, Dave Halkett, and his bride, had also had a homestead nearby before moving to town. Kris Iverson, originally from Denmark, came over the trail to settle in this area. The Holt brothers, Sam, Bill and Ed, and their cousin Harry Clarke, came from County Kildare, Ireland. There were many others, including our parents, who were from Eastern Canada or the United States. There were Longs, Bieraugels, Camerons, Armstrongs, Ridleys, and many others.

Mother had especially enjoyed the week of her sister and brother-in-law's stay. It had been both a break for her and a reunion with her sister. Before this, because of their early separation, she had never felt close to Eve. Mother was the steady one and, unlike Eve, made friends for life. And although she was the best looking of the two, she could not help envying Eve her sparkling personality and flirtatious nature which attracted both men and women to her like bees to a honey tree.

A few months after Aunt Eve and Uncle Carl left, in October, Grandma and Edward returned to Calgary. A bad flu was making the rounds at the time. I remember Mother's white face when she called Carlton and me outside, saying, "If ever I needed your help, it's now." She told us to move all perishable food from the house to the empty bunkhouse and to keep the three younger ones outside, as she intended pouring formaldehyde onto live coals to fumigate the house. It was a good thing we were not there to see the result. The fumes knocked her out cold. She admitted later that in her haste she had been reckless. After pouring a generous amount on the fire, she leaned over the smoldering coals and inhaled deeply to make sure the formaldehyde had not lost its strength. Ten minutes later, she opened her eyes and found herself lying on the floor. It worked though. Only Dad got the flu!

Dad's flu added to Mother's work. As he did not approve of women doing barn work, he had never taught Mother to milk, and now she had to rely on the neighbours, but she made the deliveries herself. She did enjoy delivering the milk to town, even if it meant taking all of us along. H.A. George helped us out by recommending a man who was looking for a job. A recent arrival from Scotland, he had grown up on a dairy farm. Scottie McNab did not like children, and we did not like this taciturn Scot, whose broad accent made it hard for us to understand him. He certainly knew his job though, and Dad kept him on long after he recovered.

We children had no idea how worn and depressed Mother had become. But it was not until Grandma and Edward left that a feeling of restless dissatisfaction engulfed my Mother. We returned home from school one wintery day to discover that Mother had left, taking Warren and Marjory with her. Dad said that she needed a rest and had gone to be with Grandma in Calgary. In response to our questioning, Dad told us in a cross voice that we were too young to understand. We were frightened, and when Junior cried in the night I crawled into bed with my brothers and, although we shed a few tears, we were soon asleep.

Our days were mostly bleak and dreary during that time. Not only did we need our mother, we also missed our brother and baby sister. To make matters worse, our good-natured father became morose and harsh, expecting us to cook and do many of Mother's tasks. He even spanked Carlton for not sweeping the rug properly. We hated this task, as clouds of dust filled the air while we swept.

Mother was probably away for only a few weeks, but it seemed a long time to us. I was shocked to discover years later, when she tried to explain why she changed her mind and came back, that she had intended to leave for good. If we children had known she had intended staying away, we would have been devastated. Warren's tonsillitis, she said, saved her from making a terrible mistake. When he became delirious from a high fever and she thought she was going to lose him, she realized how much she needed her family. After Warren recovered, his doctor advised her to take him home because he was not used to heated buildings. About then, she received a sad letter from Carlton, saying if she was not back soon we would all be as thin as stove pipes. Then, like the first songbird in the spring, we heard Dad's happy whistle. Mother would be home on the next train, setting our world aright again.

Looking back, I often picture Mother sewing by the fire, the soft lamplight making a golden halo of her hair. For years she had dressed us from the trousseau she had hardly worn. With four pregnancies in six years, she had not much use for lovely garments. Her long full petticoats with flounces of eyelet embroidery, became my pretty dresses, Carlton's shirts, and baby clothes for the younger children. Even our winter clothes were made from suits and coats she could no longer wear. One of her accomplishments was a fuzzy beaver bonnet for me from a wide-brimmed hat that had been her pride and joy.

I was not happy until she taught me to sew. It must have been quite a nuisance – threading my needle and untangling the thread. But her patience and my persistence finally paid off. I was fourteen before I was allowed to make a dress for myself, and it was made from one of hers at that. I have a photograph of myself on a brochure for my first major showing of my self-taught "Fabric Art" hangings, held at the Ottawa National Museum of Natural Science. To my family's astonishment, as well as my own, many exhibitions followed. My only regret was that my mother was not able to see the results of her early training.

After we had moved to our new farm and my parents owed money to the bank as well as the mortgage company, it was Mother's duty to see that we all helped with the work. But there were times when she would let the mortgage go hang. One such occasion was the Christmas the Peace River Public and High School gave a party for its students. The West Peace River School had recently closed, making it necessary for Carlton and me to attend school in town. I was lucky having Miss Effie Algar for my teacher. I had missed much school during those first two years and I needed help. Although she had been kind and helpful from the first, it was a story that I wrote that intrigued her. It was about a pair of scissors, a needle, and a spool of thread who got into an argument over who was the most important. Mother sent us off in our best clothes the first day, but after that, we had to wear our everyday clothes. It had never mattered what we wore to the Stewart School, we were all in the same boat. But it was not the same here. Many of the townspeople had made money, and for the first time in my life I came up against clothes snobbery.

Mother, as many other homestead women did, bleached out

and dyed flour sacks for some of my dresses. She could not get all the markings out and they showed through. My feelings were hurt when a couple of the girls started whispering and giggling behind my back. When I was reluctant to go to the Christmas party, Mother guessed my reason. I'll never know how she managed it, but with her second-hand sewing machine she made me a beautiful red velvet dress.

While everyone was waiting in the hall for the party to begin, Mr. Russell, our principal, who had helped Carlton and me find our rooms on our first day, came up to me and admired my new dress. He said that I reminded him of his little girl who was a year younger than I. Taking a photo from his wallet, he showed me a picture of a girl who did look like me.

I was only allowed to wear my red velvet dress for special occasions, but from then on no one noticed my everyday dresses.

CHAPTER TWENTY-ONE

Shaftsbury Trail

It was a beautiful morning in the first week of May. It had been a long, cold winter and spring was late. In the fields behind the cattle shed, the slowly melting snow revealed patches of rich black earth. The lilting chirp of a robin joined the noise of crows. The snow melted down a few more inches as the sun climbed higher in the sky. Nothing could have taken the joy from my heart nor the spring from my step that wonderful morning – for this was moving day.

We had all been up since daylight, packing a big lunch, lugging out our precious belongings, and stowing them away in the hayrack of one of the sleighs or in the grain box of the other one. My dad, the hired man, and my brother Carlton fed the livestock and turned them into the pasture until we returned that night.

I had never seen my parents so happy. They knew, of course, that the mortgage payments on the new place would not be easy to meet, but life had not been easy for them ever since they left Edmonton nine years earlier in a covered sleigh, to make their way over frozen muskeg and lakes in the bitter cold of our northern winter, with an eighteen-month-old and me to be born six months later.

However, that story has already been told.

We all piled into the sleighs that bright May morning. I was a tomboy and I wanted to join Carlton and Wilbur and the hired man and perch high up on the hayrack. However, I had found my mother in tears as she looked around our nearly empty little cabin and decided to stay with her and help with my little brother Warren and baby sister Marjory.

I could not understand her being sad until I glanced down at the old pond at the bottom of the hill. The water on the ice turned it blue and sparkling, and I thought of the fun we had had poling around on our little raft. I knew, too, that we would not be going to sleep to the tune of the frogs croaking, ever again. However, I was only nine years old and soon the excitement of moving overcame me again. We were on our way to a new life; we would be going to school in town and could attend Sunday School, too. I had heard Mother put forth these arguments and many more as she encouraged Dad to borrow and scrape in order to raise money for the down payment. It had really been too far to deliver milk in a horse drawn vehicle, and this new farm on the Shaftsbury Trail, just four miles from town, seemed to be the answer.

We were on our way to a new life and Dad was singing an old song, "There's a Long, Long Trail Awinding." Nothing could spoil our adventure this day. It was nearly ten miles to our new home and we should not have delayed, but, with neighbours coming out and wishing us well as we passed by, the sun was getting very hot and the snow, as we descended the long hills into the valley, was starting to melt.

The glorious smell of spring made us lighthearted. Pussy willows were turning from pinkish grey to fluffy yellow. The sticky buds of the poplars looked ready to burst into leaf. Misery Mountain, the huge hill that circled the back of our ranch, was dotted with crocuses.

We approached a house with huge fields on either side. This was the Putras' place and later became part of our land. Several mares with their long-legged colts came near the fence to look at us. The field to the left ended at the bottom of Misery. We turned and followed along the other field until the road came out on a wooded area that ended at the top of the hill. As we looked down, our eyes met a view so breathtakingly beautiful that we forgot our worries in the joy that all this would be part of our new home.

The land fell to the river in large plateaus. On the left, a little field used for a pasture was bordered by a creek with giant spruce, poplar, and birch trees. On the right was a spruce grove, with paths made by the horses, although a family of deer left their footprints along them. The next level was where the St. Germains had built their home, a home that was now to be ours. The big barn to the right and the horse barn to the left were separated by a road. The St. Germains had allowed the road to go through their land, as they ran a stopping place here during the Yukon gold rush.

The large, two-storeyed house, surrounded by big maple trees, was set to the left on a hill overlooking the river. It had a gabled roof and a veranda in the front. Another, larger house stood behind it and two smaller buildings nearby. It looked like a village to us, compared to the little log cabin, barn, and cattle sheds we had left behind.

The Shaftsbury Trail wound below the house with fields on the other side. Beyond the fields flowed the mighty Peace River. The junction of the Smoky River billowed on the far side. The Smoky was narrow compared to the Peace and had many rapids.

As we proceeded down to the next level, Misery Mountain loomed above us, its steep grassy hills rising in folds, one above the other, hundreds of feet high. They were softened by gullies, with pockets of trees and berry bushes growing along their edges. Fairly wide trails made by buffalo criss-crossed the lower slopes.

We came around the corner of the horse barn, and discovered that the St. Germains were ready to leave with the last of their belongings. My dad got down from the sleigh and introduced himself to a man, who turned out to be one of the grown sons, and his family. They later became our friends, but for the time being they considered us in the same category as the mortgage company that, they felt, had dealt with them unjustly. This made my parents unhappy, and an even greater sadness met us later.

My mother and I climbed upstairs while exploring the house and looked out the back window. There we could see Mrs. St.

Germain, a tiny Métis woman, standing under four big maple trees in the back yard. Her apron was flung over her head to hide the tears, but we could hear her sobs. We discovered later, when we buried our dear baby brother Keith under those same maple trees, that a little St. Germain baby had also been buried there. We had little to say as we made our way slowly back to the homestead. Our parents happiness was dimmed by another family's misfortune.

As I crawled under our quilts that night, I thought of the wonders this day had brought. Somehow our future had become linked with the past: with the ancient river seen from its high banks, with huge chunks of ice piled high on either side; with the big buck deer lying serenely just visible over the first knoll on Misery with only his head and shoulders showing, and behind him, barely visible, a small doe; with the stars that shone down on us all.

In the years to follow, Misery Mountain became an extension of our home. Spring meant climbing it to look for the first crocus, or riding horseback over it to look for our cattle. In the summer, we went for walks along the trail that followed the creek around the bottom of the mountain, under shady spruce trees. And in the fall when the saskatoons were ripe, Dad and Mother and we children, lard pails tied to our belts, again followed the trails. If it was a good season, we got enough of these juicy berries for my mother to put up to last all winter. When we climbed to the very top of the mountain, we felt the whole world was at our feet, for we could see the town of Peace River in the distance, surrounded by its hills. If we concentrated hard enough, we could see a grain elevator at the top of the Judah Hill opposite. The river below us wound between hills and valleys, islands and sand bars dotted here and there on its broad back.

That was half a century ago, and our little brother Keith still lies side-by-side with the St. Germain baby. We other children have spread far and wide, to return now and then to the place that was our home.

Afterword

This is where I intended ending my story, but like the river, the long trail did not end there. Like the river, it just branched off and widened out before going around the next bend. It is hard to imagine the difference those few miles made.

Life was still a struggle, as Dad figured and worried and juggled the bank loan and told himself and Mother that next year they would break even. He did well enough with his milk delivery. He studied the scientific way to handle milk. Besides keeping everything sterile, he learned the necessity of plunging his cans of milk immediately into ice cold water to remove the animal heat. To accomplish this, he built a wooden sluice to carry water into his milkhouse from a spring over five hundred yards away. He laughed when he heard the rumour that he was using chemicals to keep his milk sweet – and he beat out the opposition operating from a motor van.

Never was there a happier man than my father as he strode over his fields and watched his cattle lift their heads in trusting curiosity as he came to bring them in. The land was his, and in all his life he had never known such a feeling of accomplishment. It was twelve years before Dad could be persuaded to take a trip away from the farm, and only then to attend the Calgary Stampede where he proudly watched my brother Wilbur win the belt in Wild Bronco Busting, at the age of eighteen.

The farm was beginning to do well when the Depression hit.

But with Dad's many projects and Mother's resourcefulness, they pulled through. The year Wainwright was hailed out, Mother persuaded Dad to let her take a freight car full of potatoes to this district. She managed to sell the lot. But, as Dad often said, "Your Mother could sell ashes to the devil."

Two more children were added to our family: Keith, who lived for a short while, and Donald Floyd, born a year later. He was a great joy to us all, but to me especially. Mother was very busy and, as I was now thirteen, I became his willing slave.

Four years later, when Donnie learned that I was soon to be married, he was a bit upset. My wily Ged made a deal with him, buying me for ten pennies. When we returned after our honeymoon, a sad little boy met us with ten pennies clutched in his small grubby hand: he wanted his Beulah back!

Like many families, my parents watched their three sons and sons-in-law go off to war. And although Carlton was wounded in Italy, he, along with Wilbur and Ged, came home safely. Warren was shot down over France after volunteering as a Pathfinder. This squad's dangerous mission was to fly ahead of the bombers and drop flares over strategic enemy supplies so that the bombers, following them, could zero in. Mother never quite recovered from losing him. While in her late seventies, her memory slipped away.

Dad lived to the ripe old age of ninety-four. He was buried on the knoll above the creek, with old Misery towering above and a view of the mighty Peace below. As Ged and I drove out for his burial that beautiful fall day, I could almost hear Dad chuckle, "By golly, the kids really did it up right this time."

Six years later, Mother was laid to rest beside him. Although we knew that their spirits were free to be anywhere, it was a comfort to know we had chosen the place they had loved while here on earth. Like so many stalwart pioneers who helped settle this great country, they had come to the end of their long trail.